Unpacking Metaphor-related Prepositions in Political Discourse

This book explores the context around why English prepositions are used in figurative language more frequently than nouns and verbs, using corpus-based evidence to examine the most often used prepositions and how they are employed and for what purpose.

While research on cognitive approaches to metaphor has significantly expanded in recent decades, little attention has been paid to prepositions as vehicles of figurative language, owing to their polysemous, complex, and inconsistent nature. To bridge this gap, Ounis introduces an innovative conceptual framework that integrates conceptual metaphor theory, diachronic linguistics, and discourse pragmatics. Drawing upon an extensive corpus of American presidential inaugural addresses, this book considers the linguistic, conceptual, pragmatic, and contextual dimensions of English prepositions, revealing the fascinating interplay between language, culture, and cognition.

This volume will be of interest to scholars in pragmatics, metaphor studies, English language, rhetoric studies, and historical linguistics.

Mokhtar Ounis is a linguist who earned his PhD from the University of Toulon in France, where he conducted research on the use of conceptual metaphors in political communication. He has been a faculty member at the University of Hail in Saudi Arabia for ten years, where he has taught courses in linguistics and related fields.

Routledge Research on New Waves in Pragmatics
Series Editors: Istvan Kecskes, University at Albany, SUNY, USA and Monika Kirner-Ludwig, University of Innsbruck, Austria

Fresh Perspectives on Major Issues in Pragmatics
Edited by Monika Kirner-Ludwig

Discourse Markers in Second Language French
Alisha Reaves

Unpacking Metaphor-related Prepositions in Political Discourse
From Polysemous to Powerful
Mokhtar Ounis

The Pragmatics of Multiword Terms
The Impact of Context
Melania Cabezas-García

For more information about this series, please visit: https://www.routledge.com/Routledge-Research-on-New-Waves-in-Pragmatics/book-series/RRNWP

Unpacking Metaphor-related Prepositions in Political Discourse
From Polysemous to Powerful

Mokhtar Ounis

NEW YORK AND LONDON

First published 2024
by Routledge
605 Third Avenue, New York, NY 10158

and by Routledge
4 Park Square, Milton Park, Abingdon, Oxon, OX14 4RN

Routledge is an imprint of the Taylor & Francis Group, an informa business

© 2024 Mokhtar Ounis

The right of Mokhtar Ounis to be identified as author of this work has been asserted in accordance with sections 77 and 78 of the Copyright, Designs and Patents Act 1988.

All rights reserved. No part of this book may be reprinted or reproduced or utilised in any form or by any electronic, mechanical, or other means, now known or hereafter invented, including photocopying and recording, or in any information storage or retrieval system, without permission in writing from the publishers.

Trademark notice: Product or corporate names may be trademarks or registered trademarks, and are used only for identification and explanation without intent to infringe.

Library of Congress Cataloging-in-Publication Data
Names: Ounis, Mokhtar, author.
Title: Unpacking metaphor-related preposition in political discourse : from polysemous to powerful / Mokhtar Ounis.
Description: New York, NY : Routledge, 2024. |
Series: Routledge research on new waves in pragmatics | Originally presented as the author's thesis (doctoral) - Toulon University, 2021. | Includes bibliographical references and index. |
Identifiers: LCCN 2023041161 | ISBN 9781032431611 (hardback) | ISBN 9781032439662 (paperback) | ISBN 9781003369646 (ebook)
Subjects: LCSH: English language—Prepositions. | Metaphor—Political aspects. | English language—Political aspects. | Communication in politics. | Presidents—United States—Inaugural addresses.
Classification: LCC PE1335 .O96 2024 | DDC 425.7—dc23/eng/20231010
LC record available at https://lccn.loc.gov/2023041161

ISBN: 9781032431611 (hbk)
ISBN: 9781032439662 (pbk)
ISBN: 9781003369646 (ebk)

DOI: 10.4324/9781003369646

Typeset in Times New Roman
by codeMantra

Dedicated to my wife Radhia: In the pages of my life, you are the most exquisite story.

Contents

Preface   *ix*

1 Introduction   1
   1.1 Defining key terms 2
   1.2 Scope of this study 3
   1.3 Structure of this book 5

2 Navigating prepositions   9
   2.1 Defining prepositions 9
   2.2 Polysemy: networks and principles 10
   2.3 Cognitive grammar's view of prepositions 12
   2.4 Prepositions' cognitive potential 14
   2.5 Prepositions' contextual dynamics 16
   2.6 Prepositions' axiological framing 17

3 Metaphor: insights from classical and cognitive approaches   21
   3.1 Classical views on metaphor 21
   3.2 Cognitive view on metaphor 27

4 The power of prepositions in political discourse   35
   4.1 Political language 35
   4.2 The history of political discourse analysis 36
   4.3 The inaugural addresses and their generic properties 39
   4.4 Conceptual metaphors in political discourse 41
   4.5 The evolution trends of inaugural addresses 43
   4.6 Metaphor variation and diachronic approach 44

viii Contents

5 A prepositional portrait: corpus and frequency   50
  5.1 Corpus linguistics and metaphor research 50
  5.2 The Inaugural Corpus 50
  5.3 The prepositions' frequency patterns 52
  5.4 Tracking the preposition-to-word ratio 55

6 Patterns of preposition-based conceptualization in inaugurals   59
  6.1 Conceptual mappings of metaphor-related prepositions 59
  6.2 System metaphors and cross-system mapping 61
  6.3 The coherence of metaphors 63
  6.4 Prepositions and their metonymic basis 66
  6.5 Conceptual notation revisited 69

7 Cognitive functions of metaphor-related prepositions in political narratives   73
  7.1 The cognitive model: an overview 73
  7.2 Conceptual identity 73
  7.3 Conceptual space 77

8 Tracing patterns of diachronic variations across the inaugurals   87
  8.1 Metaphor variations 87
  8.2 Patterns of diachronic variations 93

9 Concluding remarks   100
  9.1 How are prepositions distributed in the Inaugural Corpus? 100
  9.2 What is the conceptual basis of metaphor-related prepositions? 101
  9.3 How do metaphor-related prepositions mix? 101
  9.4 Do metaphor-related prepositions reflect any systematic conceptualizations? 102
  9.5 How do metaphor-related prepositions vary across history? 102
  9.6 Final words 103

Index   *107*

Preface

This work represents a somewhat revised version of my doctoral thesis I completed in the Doctoral College ED 509 at Toulon University in March 2021. The genesis of this research project began when I was reflecting on the art of creating effective metaphors. Specifically, I was intrigued by the idea of how skilled ghostwriters carefully select the right words and collaborate with their clients to produce speeches that captivate audiences around the world. It struck me that these writers understand the power of every single word, from the tiniest particles to the relationship between nouns.

I have always been fascinated by the intricacies of language, particularly prepositions, and how they relate to other parts of speech. However, I was surprised to discover that previous studies on metaphors had largely overlooked the role of prepositions. This realization prompted me to embark on a research journey to explore the impact of prepositions on metaphorical expressions and shed light on this underexplored area of inquiry.

There is nothing more rewarding than finding the right metaphor, the one that can make something complex accessible. In the realm of political communication, even the smallest linguistic elements, such as prepositions, are utilized to create powerful metaphors. Unfortunately, prepositions are notoriously shunned, even in their literal senses, and are seldom considered part of the metaphorical landscape.

While classic examples of metaphors such as "Richard is a lion" and "Juliet is the sun" are still admired for their poetic beauty and vividness, they rely primarily on the use of nouns. More creative metaphors may include verbs and adjectives, but how many of you remember good metaphors with prepositions?

Prepositions, like other parts of speech, are crucial tools in political discourse that enable speakers to express a broad range of conceptual metaphors. However, this seemingly straightforward statement oversimplifies the complex and interdisciplinary nature of its underlying components, which include prepositions, metaphor, political discourse, pragmatics, and diachronic variations. To gain a comprehensive understanding of the interconnections between these diverse fields, it is necessary to appreciate the nuanced concept of prepositions, the definition of metaphor and political thought, as well as the significance of pragmatics and diachronic linguistics in the study of metaphors. This book is a journey along these various paths to explore these topics and their crossroads. By the end of this journey, you will gain a deep appreciation for the beauty and power of the metaphors expressed through prepositions.

It is my pleasure to acknowledge those who have helped me to bring this work to the present form. First and foremost, I would like to express my sincere appreciation to my thesis committee, comprised of Zoltan Kövecses, Jean-Rémi Lapaire, Sandrine Sorlin, Marie Gayte Lebrun, and my advisor Richard Trim. Their invaluable guidance, encouragement, and feedback have been instrumental in shaping my research and refining my ideas. I would also like to acknowledge the invaluable contributions of Jean-Rémi Lapaire, Michèle Monte, and Richard Trim, who have provided insightful comments and suggestions during the regular assessment sessions. Their expertise and knowledge have been crucial in shaping my analysis and providing theoretical insight. Finally, I would like to acknowledge the support of my family, who have provided me with unwavering encouragement and inspiration throughout this journey.

1 Introduction

Prepositions are contentious and elusive, but they have never ceased to attract the attention of linguists. These little words that appear so frequently in both spoken and written language evoke a diverse array of meanings ranging from spatial, temporal, and various figurative extensions. Exploring these various meanings has been one of the prominent research areas within cognitive linguistics and, especially, in metaphor studies. For example, Nacey (2010: 271) conducted a corpus-based analysis of a 40,000-word corpus and found that "an average of 75% of the total numbers of prepositions are metaphorically related words". While this percentage is impressive on its own, it becomes even more remarkable, considering that Nacey's corpus comprised texts written by English language learners. When they are metaphorically used, prepositions do not "stand out from other words in the sentence" (Trim 2011: 176) and can be classified as "covertly persuasive metaphors", according to the same researcher. Nacey's finding and Trim's remark not only highlight the pervasiveness of prepositions in figurative language and their covert nature but also prompt a wider investigation into the usage of such prepositions in larger and more authentic corpora.

Despite their cognitive value, rhetorical power, and pragmatic efficacy, prepositions have received relatively little attention (Matlock 2012: 483). In metaphor studies, researchers tended to favor content words, such as nouns and verbs, at the expense of prepositions. For example, Cameron (2007) explains that the identification of prepositions in their figurative senses is difficult when employing traditional methods of metaphor identification. These methodological difficulties, among other reasons, have contributed to the under-exploration of prepositional metaphors, resulting in a significant gap in our understanding of how language reflects our conceptualizations of social and political issues. Consequently, there is a pressing need for research that can dedicate adequate attention to metaphor-related prepositions supported by empirical and corpus-based evidence. To address this research gap, this book explores the use of prepositions in their figurative senses in the Inaugural Corpus, consisting of the American inaugural addresses (hereafter referred to as "inaugurals").

DOI: 10.4324/9781003369646-1

These addresses represent "the most visible component of president power" in the most solemn event of any president's life (Collier 2014: 3). This power is expressed through language as each incoming president uses the inaugural address to communicate their political thoughts to the whole nation and the global community. Effective communication is expected to persuade, and good presidents are expected to embody the notion that the "presidential power is the power to persuade", as Neustadt (1991: 11) affirms. More specifically, presidents persuade through "their command of rhetoric and their skill in using metaphor" (Charteris-Black 2011: 1). Metaphor, in particular, serves as a powerful tool for presidents to connect with their audience on an emotional level and mobilize support for their policies. Nevertheless, the question at hand is not whether to employ a metaphor or not, but how to select the most fitting metaphor. Within the context of crafting an inaugural address, this becomes a crucial task, considering that each address is supposed to be "the most carefully written and elaborately rehearsed speech of any president's career" (Fields 1996: 114). Speechwriters should have sufficient expertise to select the parts of speech that best express the linguistic metaphors they want to communicate to the public. It goes without saying that even prepositions are carefully selected to ensure that a political text exerts its power and compels "the world conform to its words" (Oakley 2005: 446).

By way of example, consider the following:

1) "And so, my fellow Americans: ask not what your country can do for you--ask what you can do for your country" (Kennedy 1961).

In (1), the preposition FOR plays a crucial role in both the metaphorical meaning and the rhetorical impact of President Kennedy's memorable words. By defining and redefining the relationship between the people and their country, FOR establishes new roles for both entities, where the people become benefactors rather than beneficiaries.

As I shall argue and demonstrate, prepositions can, in the hands of an experienced communicator, be a powerful tool for shaping meaning and influencing audience perception.

Before delving into analysis, it is crucial to address the main concern of selecting the appropriate terminology to be consistently used throughout this book. More precisely, we have to address the following question: how should we refer to prepositions when they are used in their figurative senses?

1.1 Defining key terms

Understanding the use of prepositions in metaphorical expressions is relatively straightforward, but finding the precise term to describe such prepositions can pose a challenge. Should we refer to them as prepositional metaphors or metaphorical prepositions? The first term follows the structure of a prepositional phrase, denoting a metaphor that uses or contains a preposition. On the other hand, the second term describes cases when a preposition is used in a figurative sense, indicating a departure from its basic literal meaning. This implies that prepositions have distinct literal meanings that must be distinguished from their figurative senses. However, the reality is that prepositions are not inherently literal or metaphorical on their own. Consequently, labeling them as literal prepositions or metaphorical prepositions might lead to confusion.

In the literature, various terms have been suggested to refer to prepositions used in metaphorical expressions. For example, Sullivan (2007: 118–133) referred to them as "metaphoric preposition phrase constructions". Nacey (2010) consistently used the term "metaphorical preposition" throughout her book, while Nickels (2013) chose the term "prepositional metaphors". Other terms, such as metaphorical prepositions and relational metaphors, are also used. The diverse labels assigned to the same linguistic construction indicate an inconsistency and confusion in terminology.

These terms reflect a tradition in which metaphors are categorized based on parts of speech. However, it is important to note that this tradition comprises only three categories: nouns, verbs, and adjectives while excluding prepositions. The first category, which uses nouns as their metaphorical basis, is known as "nominal metaphors". In the second category, verbs form its metaphorical basis and generate predicate metaphors. The third and final category, which consists of adjective-based metaphors, is known as "attributive metaphors". Considering this pattern, metaphors expressed by prepositions should be called "prepositional metaphors".

To avoid such confusion and maintain clarity and consistency with the technical terminology provided by the Pragglejaz Group[1] (Steen et al. 2010), I prefer to use the term "metaphor-related prepositions" throughout this book. Metaphor identification procedures, according to this group, aim to decide whether a given word is related to metaphor or not. If it is related, it is called "a metaphor-related word" (Steen et al. 2010: 14). Following the same pattern, when a preposition is identified as related to metaphor in a sentence, it will be called "a metaphor-related preposition".

Having decided on the most suitable term to describe the prepositions under investigation, the subsequent sections of this chapter will outline the various topics covered in this book.

1.2 Scope of this study

It is crucial to clarify seven key assumptions that underpin this book's vision and methodology. First, all simple prepositions, without exception, will be explored in this study. They are treated equally, regardless of their meaning, function, or frequency. Some studies focus on spatial prepositions because their authors want to explore some issues related to space and cognition. Others emphasize orientational prepositions driven by their authors' interest in power relations and hierarchical structures. However, this study seeks to understand all prepositions and how they express figurative meanings.

Second, this book is built on the assumption that prepositions cannot be studied in isolation. They are context-dependent and need to be analyzed in relation to various contextual factors. The context in which metaphor-related prepositions are used comprises the surrounding discourse or the cotext. It consists of three essential components: a preposition, an entity preceding the preposition, and an entity following it. To provide a holistic approach to studying these entities, they will be represented in the following pattern: TRAJECTOR prep LANDMARK. In short, a trajector is usually the entity that moves, a preposition is the connecting word that establishes the relationship, and a landmark is the static entity that acts as a reference point for the trajector. For example, the preposition IN in the phrase "the military and naval officers in the (*Philippine*) islands" (McKinley 1901) is to be understood in its immediate context provided by the trajectors (officers) in relation to their landmark (the islands).

Third, within this highly abstract representation, prepositions will be treated as "relators" (Merle 2017: 12) whose primary function is "to name relationships between entities" (Jamrozik & Gentner 2015). In the above example, the preposition IN acts as a relator that creates a location-based relationship between the officers and the Philippine islands.

The fourth parameter builds on the relator function, asserting that the three entities are "conceptually dependent" (Turewicz 2004: 7). This methodology is endorsed by Langacker (1987: 215), who wrote: "one cannot conceptualize interconnections without also conceptualizing the entities that they interconnect". This guiding principle shapes the approach to studying the three entities involved – a trajector, a preposition, and a landmark. It involves examining the individual conceptualization of each entity before investigating their interconnections.

The fifth parameter is about the cases when prepositions are used in metaphorical expressions. A preposition is identified and marked as metaphor-related when it connects two seemingly dissimilar entities yet succeeds in forging a meaningful relationship. An example of a metaphor expressed by a preposition is the famous phrase "the sacred fire of liberty" uttered by President Washington (1789) in his first inaugural address. This relationship between liberty and fire is interpreted as a metaphor, with the connecting preposition, OF, establishes an integrative relationship by which fire is understood in its figurative sense and conceived as an inseparable part of the abstract concept of freedom.

The sixth parameter indicates that metaphor-related prepositions do not name preexisting relationships but rather create novel relationships in a given discourse situation. In other words, these relationships do not directly mirror the physical world, but they originate from a creative and pragmatic mind seeking to communicate effectively and persuasively. Moreover, the choice of the components of this pattern (trajectors, prepositions, and landmarks) is not constrained by semantic or syntactic rules. Instead, it is driven by the "speaker choice" (Charteris-Black 2004: 10), who is engaged in intentional communication. The speaker's choice of any metaphor-related preposition reflects their construal of a given situation and reveals (a part of) their intentions. This parameter highlights that metaphor-related prepositions are built on the speaker's construal, which is far from a "neutral way of apprehending a situation" (Langacker 2010: 34).

The seventh and final parameter deals with the comprehension of metaphor-related prepositions. According to this parameter, these prepositions function as "inferential triggers" (Hernández 2012: 1761). Inferences go beyond decoding the little meanings of the prepositions in question. Instead, they are derived from a blend of image schemas, conceptual frames, and domains encapsulated within metaphor-related prepositions. Though these inferences are triggered by prepositions, they are shaped by a myriad of sociocultural and historical contextual factors.

With these seven parameters in mind, this book adopts a cognitive linguistic approach to explore all the simple prepositions in English, with a focus on their function as relators that create meaningful relationships between two semantically incongruent entities. To validate these assumptions, a corpus-based analysis will be conducted on the Inaugural Corpus, a specific corpus comprising all the inaugural addresses delivered by American presidents from 1789 to 2021. The analysis will address five issues covering the various aspects of prepositions.

The first issue focuses on frequency, examining the occurrences and distribution of prepositions across the Inaugural Corpus. The second issue pertains to the concordance of these prepositions, aiming to illustrate how prepositions are used metaphorically in these speeches and how they collocate with semantic fields. As for the third issue, the corpus-based analysis focuses on how metaphor-related prepositions mix with one another and how they interact with other metaphors and metonymies. The fourth issue is about the links between metaphorical expressions and conceptual patterns. These patterns, drawn from the recurrent instances of metaphor-related prepositions, are examined to reveal how American presidents think and reason about political topics. The fifth and final issue deals with how metaphor-related prepositions have evolved over time and examines the factors that have contributed to their evolution.

1.3 Structure of this book

This book proceeds in the following way: Chapter 2 begins with an overview of the cognitive and semantic accounts of English prepositions, with a particular emphasis on the cognitive grammar approach. Chapter 3 focuses on the concept of metaphor and starts with a historical survey of the study of metaphor, proceeding to more recent cognitive perspectives. Chapter 4 reviews the different approaches to political discourse analysis before proceeding to presidential communication and the inaugurals as a genre. Then it focuses on political metaphors and their diachronic variations. In Chapter 5 of this work, the focus shifts to research methodology and the Inaugural Corpus. It provides a comprehensive description of all the prepositions featured in the inaugurals, including their frequency rates and distribution throughout the history of the inaugurals. Chapter 6 explores the patterns that emerge from the analysis of individual metaphor-related prepositions. Additionally, it describes the ways in which prepositions can interact with one another to create coherent clusters of metaphors. It also explores the metonymic basis of the metaphors expressed by prepositions and revises the conceptual notation in order to highlight the role of prepositions in conceptual mapping. Chapter 7 introduces a tentative model based on extracted patterns of metaphorical thoughts. This model illustrates how American presidents employ metaphor-related prepositions to conceptualize political abstract entities and issues, with a particular focus on two major areas: conceptual identity and conceptual space. In Chapter 8, metaphor-related prepositions are studied in terms of their diachronic dimensions with an emphasis on the factors that have contributed to their stability and change. Finally, Chapter 9 presents conclusions from the findings presented in the preceding chapters. In addition to implications, it also puts forward potential recommendations for future research.

Metaphors are not mere phrases on a page or spoken in a public place. They have the power to move beyond language and become enactive, capable of transforming words into action (Gallagher & Lindgren 2015: 392). This book contributes to the ongoing research to understand how metaphors operate and influence people's lives. Entman (1993: 57) argues that "political elites control the framing of issues. These frames can determine just what 'public opinion' is".

Like any other text, American inaugurals are, and will always be, open to interpretations. Their "judges are not contemporaries, but, as Hegel said, history itself" (Ricœur 1973: 103). We gain wisdom from the lessons of history by conducting research and investigating even the finest detail, including prepositions. These seemingly insignificant particles will continue to provide language users with a wide range of representations of reality and should, thus, receive in-depth interpretations.

Note

1 A group of ten researchers who developed the Metaphor Identification Procedure (MIP) in 2007. The term Pragglejaz is an acronym composed of the researchers' first name initials.

References

Cameron, Lynne J. 2007. Patterns of metaphor use in reconciliation talk. *Discourse & Society* 18(2). 197–222.

Charteris-Black, Jonathan. 2004. *Corpus approaches to critical metaphor analysis*. 1st edn. New York, NY: Palgrave MacMillan.

Charteris-Black, Jonathan. 2011. *Politicians and rhetoric: The persuasive power of metaphor*. New York, NY: Palgrave MacMillan.

Collier, Ken. 2014. Rhetoric and representation: Exploring the institutionalization of presidential speechwriting. In *Southern Political Science Association Meeting*, 1–32. New Orleans, LA: Southern Political Science Association.

Entman, Robert Mathew. 1993. Framing: Toward clarification of a fractured paradigm. *Journal of Communication* 43(4). 51–58.

Fields, Wayne. 1996. *Union of words: A history of presidential eloquence*. New York, NY: Free Press.

Gallagher, Shaun & Robb Lindgren. 2015. Enactive metaphors: Learning through full-body engagement. *Educational Psychology Review*. Springer 27(3). 391–404.

Hernández, Patricia. 2012. Est-on aux pizzas comme on est aux casseroles? Sur les emplois métonymiques des syntagmes prépositionnels en à avec un nom d'objet. In *SHS Web of Conferences*, vol. 1, 1759–1776.

Jamrozik, Anja & Dedre Gentner. 2015. Well-hidden regularities: Abstract uses of in and on retain an aspect of their spatial meaning. *Cognitive Science Society* 39(8). 1881–1911.

Kennedy, John F. 1961. First Inaugural Address. *The American Presidency Project*. https://www.presidency.ucsb.edu/documents/inaugural-address-2 (24 January, 2017).

Langacker, Ronald W. 1987. *Foundations of cognitive grammar: Theoretical prerequisites*. Vol. 1. Stanford, CA: Stanford university press.

Langacker, Ronald W. 2010. Conceptualization, symbolization, and grammar. *International Journal of Cognitive Linguistics* 1(1). 31–63.

Matlock, Teenie. 2012. Framing political messages with grammar and metaphor. How something is said may be as important as what is said. *American Scientist* 100. 478–483.

McKinley, William. 1901. Second Inaugural Address. *The American Presidency Project*. https://www.presidency.ucsb.edu/documents/inaugural-address-44 (24 January, 2017).

Merle, Jean-Marie. 2017. Les prépositions en contexte. Approche de la théorie des opérations prédicatives et énonciatives (TOPE). *Corela* HS-(22). 1–12.

Nacey, Susan. 2010. *Comparing linguistic metaphors in L1 and L2 English*. [Doctoral dissertation, University of Oslo].

Neustadt, Richard E. 1991. *Presidential power and the modern presidents: The politics of leadership from Roosevelt to Reagan*. New York, NY: The Free Press.

Nickels, Edelmira L. 2013. *Metaphors in congressional discourse: Cognitive frames of the political status of Puerto Rico*. [Doctoral dissertation, Indiana University].

Oakley, Todd. 2005. Force-dynamic dimensions of rhetorical effect. In Hampe, Beate (ed.), *From perception to meaning: Image schemas in cognitive linguistics*, 443–473. Berlin, Germany: Mouton de Gruyter.

Ricœur, Paul. 1973. The model of the text: Meaningful action considered as a text. *New Literary History* 5(1). 91–117.

Steen, Gerard J., Aletta G. Dorst, J. Berenike Herrmann, Anna Kaal, Tina Krennmayr & Trijntje Pasma. 2010. *A method for linguistic metaphor identification: From MIP to MIPVU*. Amsterdam, The Netherlands: John Benjamins Publishing.

Sullivan, Karen. 2007. *Grammar in metaphor: A construction grammar account of metaphoric language*. [Doctoral dissertation, University of California].

Trim, Richard. 2011. *Metaphor and the historical evolution of conceptual mapping*. Basingstoke, England: Palgrave Macmillan.

Turewicz, Kamila. 2004. Understanding prepositions through Cognitive Grammar. A case of in. In Turewicz, Kamila (ed.), *Cognitive linguistics: A user-friendly approach*, 101–126. Szczecin: Wydawnictwo Naukowe US.

Washington, George. 1789. First Inaugural Address. *The American Presidency Project*. https://www.presidency.ucsb.edu/documents/inaugural-address-16 (24 January, 2017).

2 Navigating prepositions

2.1 Defining prepositions

Prepositions form a distinct category in English with their own grammatical functions, roles, and properties. Like other parts of speech, prepositions have specific characteristics that govern their usage and relationship to other words within a sentence. To comprehend these characteristics, this section will examine several definitions extracted from dictionaries and grammar textbooks. To highlight the distinctive features of prepositions, specific words will be italicized in a range of senses offered by dictionaries, a–e:

a   "A word or phrase placed typically *before* a substantive and indicating the *relation* of that substantive to a verb, an adjective, or another substantive" (Heritage).
b   "A word that comes *before* a noun, pronoun, or the '-ing' form of a verb, and shows its *relation* to another part of the sentence" (Macmillan).
c   "A word that is used *before* a noun, a noun phrase, or a pronoun, *connecting* it to another word" (Cambridge).
d   "A function word that typically *combines* with a noun phrase to form a phrase which usually expresses a modification or predication" (Merriam-Webster).
e   "A word governing, and usually *preceding*, a noun or pronoun and expressing a *relation* to another word or element in the clause" (Oxford).

These dictionary entries consistently highlight two main characteristics of prepositions: first, their position within a sentence, and second, their function. Prepositions are defined based on their location in relation to other entities within the sentence. Three out of the five definitions incorporate the term "before", while the fourth definition employs the term "preceding" to emphasize that this positional aspect is intrinsic to the meaning of the preposition.

The etymology of the word "preposition" underscores its inherent emphasis on position. Its origins trace back to the Latin term *praeponere*, which combines the prefix *prae*, denoting "before" or "in front of", with the verb *ponere*, meaning "to place" or "to put". As such, a preposition signifies an element intended to be positioned before or placed in front of another entity within a sentence.

In addition to their positional aspect, prepositions have another distinct feature: their function. Both dictionaries and grammar textbooks define prepositions by the function of creating a relation between two entities within a sentence. For example, Quirk et al. (1985: 657) assert that "a preposition expresses a *relation* between two entities, one being that represented by the prepositional complement, the other by another part of the sentence". Additionally, the *Longman Grammar of Spoken and Written English*, a classical grammar reference, defines a preposition as "mortar which *binds* [the main building blocks of] texts together" (Biber et al. 1999: 55).

When these two aspects are combined, a preposition signifies an entity intended to be positioned before another entity while simultaneously establishing a relationship between the preceding entity and the succeeding entity.

While these two dimensions distinguish a preposition from other parts of speech, they alone are insufficient to fully define its precise meaning. The question arises: is the meaning of a preposition independent or contingent on the relations it establishes, or is it a combination of both? Regarding the first view, it posits that a preposition possesses a fundamental semantic value that is accompanied by a constellation of interconnected meanings. Alternatively, the second view posits that prepositions derive their meanings through their semantically related associations and that these meanings can be accurately determined and anticipated via computational means, as explained by Srikumar and Roth (2013). Lastly, the third perspective blends these divergent views and elaborates a unified theory, designated as the "principled polysemy model" (Tyler & Evans 2003: 228).

2.2 Polysemy: networks and principles

Prepositions are widely recognized for their inherent polysemy, as they are not conventionally paired to specific meanings. The multiple meanings associated with each preposition may appear unrelated at first glance, but according to Tyler and Evans (2003: 237), they are not. They propose a model that outlines four principles governing the polysemy of prepositions.

According to the first principle, each preposition has a primary sense and evokes a proto-scene which "refers to what is represented in the human conceptual system" (Tyler & Evans 2003: 230). This scene is shaped by both the prepositions' geometric attributes and functions. This view is in line with Garrod, Ferrier, and Campbell (1999: 167), who argue that prepositional relationships are "best represented in terms of an inherently dynamic functional geometry". Similarly, Langacker (2010: 14) contends that "spatial and interactive considerations are closely bound up with one another, even to the point being indissociable".

Second, a proto-scene is not entirely predetermined or entirely objective. Instead, it is a composite of a spatial configuration coupled with a particular preposition developed through a high frequency of associations. For instance, a physical scene can be described with various prepositions depending on various dimensions of construal.

Third, it is worth noting that certain metaphorical relationships established by prepositions are motivated by the concepts of "experiential correlation" and "conceptual binding", as advocated by Grady (1997). Consequently, when two experiences are frequently associated, a conventional correlation between them is created, giving rise to a conceptual metaphor. "At this point in its evolution, the base term is polysemous, having both a domain-specific meaning and a related domain-general meaning" (Gentner et al. 2001). A typical example is the preposition IN, which evokes a correlation between physical locations and emotional states. Both locations and emotions are considered primary scenes, which give rise to primary metaphors, as Grady (1997: 26) asserts. This correlation between physical locations and emotional states becomes entrenched and gives rise to the STATES ARE LOCATIONS metaphor. Consequently, a preposition gradually acquires a metaphorical meaning through entrenched conceptual mapping.

The fourth and final principle of Tyler and Evans's model pertains to pragmatic inferencing. Language users typically create relationships between entities by using at least three inferencing strategies, namely "best fit", "knowledge of real-world force dynamics", and "topological extension". As for the first strategy, people tend to choose the preposition that provides "the best fit between the conceptual spatial relation and the speaker's communicative needs" (Tyler & Evans 2003: 57). This strategy is grounded in relevance theory, which asserts that a message should be encoded with "optimal relevance" (Wilson & Sperber 2017: 2) and that "human cognition tends to be geared to the maximization of relevance" (Sperber & Wilson 1996: 260). The second strategy is about the real-world knowledge we activate in either producing or processing prepositional relationships. Finally, the third strategy accounts for the extensible nature of prepositions. While the relationships between spatial entities may appear fixed, they are actually subject to a wide range of extensions. These relationships can be extended to cover abstract domains without violating their geometric attributes and functions.

These four principles are meant to explain the polysemous semantic network of prepositions. However, Tyler and Evans's model is restricted to spatial particles and does not include other prepositions. Thus, a thorough understanding of prepositions requires a broader theoretical framework that goes beyond polysemy and spatial relationships. Cognitive grammar, as proposed by Langacker, offers foundational concepts and insightful guidelines.

2.3 Cognitive grammar's view of prepositions

Cognitive grammar considers prepositions, along with other parts of speech, as meaningful units that constitute an integral part of our conceptual system. These units aid in generating and evoking our conceptualizations whenever "we engage the world at many levels: physical, mental, social, cultural, emotional, and imaginative" (Langacker 2008a: 10). During this conceptualizing process, we view the human experience through two distinct realms: the active and the circumstantial. In the active realm, human participants interact with the world and have an impact on the circumstances that arise in the present and future. The circumstantial realm, on the other hand, pertains to "settings, locations, and static situations, where objects with stable properties are arranged in particular ways" (Langacker 2010: 8).

Prepositions are the grammatical categories that are "canonically used for describing stable situations in the circumstantial realm" (Langacker 2010: 10). However, these categories can characterize not only the spatial relationships within the circumstantial realm but also the actions taken by humans and their effects on this realm. In other words, prepositions create relations between participants in the active realm and settings in the circumstantial realm. These relations provide insight into how human actions affect circumstances and, in turn, are influenced by them.

In most relationships designated by prepositions, an agent and a setting become interconnected. The agent is the primary focal entity, while the setting is the secondary entity. These entities are arranged in a hierarchical relationship, with the focus entity referred to as "the trajector" and the reference entity as "the landmark". The trajector, typically smaller and movable, takes the foreground, while the landmark, often larger and stationary, remains in the background.

When a preposition connects these two entities, it "specifies a region in space, characterized in relation to the landmark object, within which the trajector can be found" (Langacker 2010: 12). This means that prepositions convey information not only about the location of the trajector but also about its relationship to the landmark object. To provide a concrete example of this relationship, let us consider the same sentence but with three different prepositions:

1 Jill is *in* the garage.
2 Jill is *on* the garage.
3 Jill is *near* the garage.

The prepositions in (1)–(3) specify the relationship between an active realm, represented by the agent, Jill, and a circumstantial realm, represented by the setting, the garage. The landmark is "invoked, not as a location in and of itself, but rather as a point of reference for defining one" (Langacker 2010: 12). More precisely, it is the preposition that determines the specific point of reference in relation to the landmark within which Jill is found. While these examples share the same landmark, namely the garage, the prepositions employed define different points of reference relative to the garage. Specifically, IN specifies the interior of the garage in (1), ON specifies the surface of the garage in (2), and NEAR specifies the vicinity of the garage in (3).

Furthermore, a preposition not only defines the area within the landmark but also employs the landmark as a means of locating the trajector. The landmark is transformed into a reference point within which the trajector can be situated and subsequently identified. To describe this process in terms related to searching and finding, the trajector is conceived as a target of search, the landmark as a reference point, and the preposition as an indicator of a search domain. Vandeloise (2017: 3) explains that the landmark serves as "a reference point localizing the target". The process of searching and finding implies a mental map by which a "conceptualizer traces the same mental path (from a reference point to search domain to target) by way of apprehending the locative relationship" (Langacker 2010: 12). Upon encountering the utterance in (1), the reader is likely to engage in two mental operations. The first operation involves locating the target, Jill, by using the garage as a reference point, followed by searching for Jill within the search domain, the garage. The second operation requires the reader to mentally trace Jill's path leading up to her current location inside the garage. Even though Jill is simply located in a setting without engaging in any physical action or exerting force upon the garage, she is still regarded as an active agent and a representative of the active realm. In this case, Jill is in an extreme attenuation, whereby she passively occupies a location, and her movement is in a degenerate state.

In addition to locating a trajector with reference to a landmark, prepositions are also understood via their function of "qualification by means of relations" (Radden & Dirven 2007: 157). By relating one entity to another, prepositions qualify both entities through two types of relations: intrinsic and schematic. The intrinsic relations, usually expressed through postnominal possessive constructions, "involve a whole and a part and are expressed by means of the preposition OF" (Radden & Dirven 2007: 158). For example, in the phrase "the roof of the house", the preposition OF expresses the intrinsic relation between a roof and a house by indicating that the roof is an integral part of the house. According to Lindstromberg (2010: 205–208), the preposition OF has an "integrative function", which makes us understand that a part (a roof) is an integral part of a whole (a house). This integrative relationship is supported by Langacker (2008b: 345), who affirms that "the trajector is an intrinsic subpart of the landmark". In this case, the trajector is understood as a unit of a mass. The existence of this unit is realized through "the unitization of a mass" (Langacker 2008b: 342) by which a specific unit is selected.

It is worth noting that, in cognitive grammar, the preposition OF is studied in terms of its intrinsic relationships rather than its possessive attributes as in traditional grammar.

In the case of schematic relations, a preposition structures the semantic content of the two interconnected entities according to a particular image schema (Tseng 2007: 138–139). The choice of preposition activates a particular image schema, which then structures the semantic content of the trajector and landmark. Radden and Dirven (2007: 160) argue that "the schematic relation is determined by the choice of the preposition". For instance, the preposition ON in the phrase "the book is on the table" evokes the SUPPORT image schema and structures the relationship between the table and the book in terms of a supporting entity and a supported entity. Another example would be the preposition IN, which evokes the CONTAINER schema. When IN connects a specific trajector to a particular landmark, it establishes a relationship in which the landmark acts as the containing entity and the trajector acts as the contained entity. Other schematic relations may involve LOCATION, DIRECTION, INCLUSION, and CONTACT, among others.

These two types of relations, namely intrinsic and schematic, are usually extended to encompass abstract connections between entities generating metonymic and metaphoric meanings.

2.4 Prepositions' cognitive potential

Prepositions are widely used in metaphorical linguistic expressions. For example, in her study of academic, news, conversations, and fiction registers, Herrmann (2013: 146) noticed that "one-third of all prepositions are related to metaphor in each register". She also observed that prepositions "have the highest proportion of metaphor of all word classes in each of the four registers" (Herrmann 2013: 182). Similarly, Deignan (1997: 329–330) noted that prepositions are highly frequent in her corpus, but she categorized them as "delexical" and consequently decided to exclude them from her research. In contrast, Sullivan (2007) included prepositional constructions as one of the five types of grammatical constructions used in communicating metaphor.

It is essential to note the special status of prepositions when used in metaphorical expressions. As they stand alone, prepositions are limited in their metaphorical uses due to their "simple spatial, force-dynamic and image-schematic meanings" (Sullivan 2007: 130). Due to these constraints, prepositions are unable to evoke abstract domains outside of their image schemas. In other words, prepositions are restricted to a limited number of image-schematic concepts such as "verticality, horizontality, place, region, inclusion, contact, support, gravity, attachment, dimensionality (point, line, plane or volume), distance, movement, and path" (Bowerman 1996: 422). As a result, they cannot activate concepts like emotions, arguments, or even concrete concepts like building (Sullivan 2007: 131). Instead, these concepts are activated by the semantically rich entities related by a preposition rather than by the preposition itself. When a preposition is used metaphorically, its image-schematic structure must align with the semantics of both the source and target domains to create coherent and meaningful sentences.

These constraints may be beneficial as they enhance the compatibility of prepositions with a wide range of conceptual domains compared to other parts of speech. As noted by Sullivan (2007: 74), this characteristic allows prepositions to be utilized metaphorically "in almost any context". In general, the flexible metaphoricity of prepositions can be attributed to two factors. First, prepositions are highly abstract, enabling them to fit into any context without relying on semantic valence. For instance, the preposition IN can relate to a broad range of entities as long as one entity can function as a container and the other can function as a containee. To create a containment relationship, "a minimum of two objects is required: a container and a containee" (Hedblom 2019: 111). Therefore, the high degree of abstractness allows prepositions to be used in a wide range of contexts without being obstructed by semantic constraints. The second factor that contributes to the flexibility of prepositions in metaphor is their suitability for effective "information packaging" (Biber et al. 1999). Specifically, A CONCEPT + PREPOSITION + A CONCEPT creates a denser and more complex form of referential information. When two seemingly incongruent concepts are connected by a preposition, a new referential realm emerges shaped by the schematic structure of the linking preposition. This process activates at least two mental spaces and generates a blend, as proposed by the Conceptual Integration Theory. Unlike other linguistic elements, prepositions are highly flexible and not constrained by predetermined characteristics when performing this type of blending in a concise and package-like fashion.

In addition to establishing metaphorical relationships, prepositions evoke metonymies in three different ways. In the first and second ways, a trajector or landmark, respectively, provides mental access to a conceptual domain. The third way is when a preposition's image schema has a metonymic structure, as is the case with the preposition OF. For example, in her study on the French preposition À followed by an object, Hernández (2012) observed that an object, when used as a landmark, usually acts as an entity that stands for an activity (at the piano), an entity that stands for production (at the pizza), or an entity that stands for a stage in the evolution process (at the shredded carrots).

In addition to their metaphoric and metonymic dimensions, prepositions have analogical functions. Although prepositions and analogies are distinct concepts, they share a relational nature, which explains why preposition-based metaphors are used in analogical reasoning. This type of reasoning is defined as "the ability to find and exploit similarities based on *relations* (emphasis in original) among entities, rather than solely on the entities themselves" (Holyoak & Stamenkovic 2018: 645). Analogies usually involve proportional reasoning across two conceptual domains, which can be represented as (A: B): (C: X). The (A: B) set refers to the source domain, while the

(C: X) set refers to the target domain. The relationship between A and B is then applied to C and X, invoking shared knowledge to draw connections and generate inferences. Holyoak and Stamenkovic (2018: 644) argue that the well-known statement "religion is the opium of the people" has an analogical nature and can be written in the form of (religion: people): (opium: addicts). This analogy entails that religion is to people as opium is to addicts. By drawing on this analogy, we can understand, think of, and reason about religion in terms of opium. Analogies that involve proportional reasoning usually give rise to metaphors known as "proportional or relational metaphors" (Gentner et al. 2001: 200). These metaphors help us understand the relationship between two conceptual domains in terms of the connections that exist between their elements, rather than just their individual attributes. These connections are typically expressed through prepositions, allowing us to generate inferences and predictions about the target domain based on our understanding of the relationships within the source domain. Within this framework, metaphor-related prepositions take advantage of their relational functions to generate "analogical mappings between domains" (Gentner et al. 2001: 201).

The cognitive status of prepositions remains incomplete without a thorough examination of the role of context in the emergence of their metaphorical meanings.

2.5 Prepositions' contextual dynamics

Prepositions' meanings are inferred from the context in which they are used. This view is in line with the premise that "words gain a local meaning" (Elimam & Chilton 2018: 30). Similarly, Szwedek (2008: 176), according to his objectivation theory, argues that the metaphorical senses of a preposition are "part of the context". Thus, a preposition acquires multiple meanings in discourse depending on the context in which it emerges. For instance, in "Jill is in poverty", poverty is conceptualized as a location, but the relationship between the landmark and the trajector can be better understood when we have sufficient information regarding the degree of Jill's poverty, her responsibility for that poverty, the prevailing discourse about poverty in Jill's community, and the prospects of overcoming this condition, among other factors. These contextual factors determine the meaning of the preposition IN, allowing us to infer that Jill can be enclosed, contained, confined, covered, or simply located within a socioeconomic class. Moreover, contextual cues can convey moral and cultural connotations with either positive or negative evaluations. For example, the preposition WITHIN can suggest an inclusive or protective attitude, while BEYOND can imply exclusion or distance. These inferences are not inherent in the prepositions themselves but rather emerge through the context in which they are used. Lu and others (2017: 263) claim that contextual cues can put the "rampant polysemy under control".

The role of context is reinforced by the revised versions of conceptual metaphor theory suggested by Kövecses (2020, 2015). Accordingly, a preposition typically appears in a complex and dynamic situation in which the choice of trajector and landmark, and their arrangement, are usually primed by contextual factors. Each instance of a preposition involves a dynamic interaction between these components, which can result in a reconfiguration or "reparamétrage" of the trajector-landmark arrangement, as Lapaire (2017: 14) suggests. Accordingly, metaphor-related prepositions generate a wide range of new configurations and reconfigurations as they are deeply embedded in context and susceptible to contextual influence.

When used in new contexts, prepositions acquire new inferences via metaphor and metonymy, a process that Traugott (1988: 413) calls "pragmatic strengthening". The inferential potential of prepositions is strengthened, thanks to their inherent interconnections with their surrounding entities and contexts. Each configuration generated by prepositions conveys an emergent conceptualization rooted in its context. More specifically, this emergent conceptualization is shaped by pragmatic efficiency and affected by diachronic saliency, meaning that it reflects the historical and cultural contexts in which they emerged. However, these conceptualizations cannot be neutral or devoid of evaluation. As (Lakoff 2006: 231–237) suggests, figurative language serves as a tool to frame and reframe everyday situations. Metaphor-related prepositions are no exception. Thanks to their evaluative nature, prepositions are used to frame and reframe situations, make value judgments, and shape our perspectives.

2.6 Prepositions' axiological framing

Metaphors are known to evoke frames, which are mental structures that help us interpret and understand the world around us. We generate these frames when we "select some aspects of a perceived reality and make them more salient" (Entman 1993: 52).

Conceptual mappings are inherently selective as they highlight a particular representation of reality along with its associated norms, values, and evaluations while downplaying other representations. In this way, metaphors are widely recognized for their "evaluative function" (Geeraerts & Cuyckens 2007). This idea is supported by axiological semantics, a linguistic framework that posits that concepts are evaluated against a structured and reliable system of norms and values.

Prepositions and other spatial expressions are essential in structuring a set of morality-related metaphors. Labels such as "orientational metaphors", "metaphorical orientations", "spatial orientations", and "spatial metaphors" (Lakoff & Johnson 1980) reflect the normative value and the significant axiological weight that prepositions carry. In technical terms, they carry an "axiological load" (Krzeszowski 1993) or "a built-in value judgment" (Barcelona 2003). In their axiological implications, spatial prepositions take advantage of their inherent locations, orientations, and directions to establish systematic mappings between spatial values and moral values. Szwedek (2014: 368) affirms that "orientation is only a medium representing value", meaning that it is the underlying value that is being mapped rather than the orientation itself. Every location in the space, whether high or low, near or far, is translated into the corresponding axiological value, which is then mapped onto value judgments imbued with social, moral, or political flavor.

Axiological evaluation is constrained by the "Axiological Invariance Principle" proposed by Krzeszowski (1993). Accordingly, all basic concepts are evaluated according to a positive or negative polarity. Pairs of opposing prepositions like IN, OUT, OVER, UNDER, WITH, and WITHOUT denote opposing orientations and meanings and, consequently, convey opposing evaluations.

It is important to recognize that these subjective evaluations and value judgments are not fixed, but instead, they vary depending on historical circumstances. As a result, they possess a historical timeline that can be traced through studying their diachronic evolution. This involves examining how language usage has changed over time, including when a particular concept or expression first appeared, how it has varied, and the factors that have contributed to these variations.

In general, English prepositions play a fundamental role in sentence construction by establishing a relational profile that creates meaningful connections between two entities. This role is highlighted in their primary senses, in either dictionaries or grammar textbooks. The relationships created by prepositions are intricately influenced by the image schematic meanings inherent in each preposition. In their figurative usages, prepositions take on the added role of framing situations and conveying axiological evaluations. These value judgments and their connotations are primed by the context in which metaphor-related prepositions emerge.

References

Barcelona, Antonio. 2003. On the plausibility of claiming a metonymic motivation for conceptual metaphor. In Barcelona, Antonio (ed.), *Metaphor and metonymy at the crossroads: A cognitive perspective*, 31–58. Berlin, Germany: Mouton de Gruyter.

Biber, Douglas, Stig Johansson, Geoffrey Leech, Susan Conrad & Edward Finegan. 1999. *The Longman grammar of spoken and written English*. London, England: Longman.

Bowerman, Melissa. 1996. Learning how to structure space for language: A crosslinguistic perspective. In Bloom, Paul, Peterson, Mary A., Nadel, Lynn & Garrett, Merril F. (ed.), *Language and space*, 383–436. Cambridge, MA: MIT Press.

Cambridge. The Cambridge English Dictionary. https://dictionary.cambridge.org/dictionary/english/preposition (20 February, 2023).

Deignan, Alice Helen. 1997. *A corpus-based study of some linguistic features of metaphor*. [Doctoral dissertation, The University of Birmingham].

Elimam, Abdou & Paul Chilton. 2018. The paradoxical hybridity of words. *Language and Cognition*. Cambridge University Press 10(2). 208–233.
Entman, Robert Mathew. 1993. Framing: Toward clarification of a fractured paradigm. *Journal of Communication* 43(4). 51–58.
Garrod, Simon, Gillian Ferrier & Siobhan Campbell. 1999. In and on: Investigating the functional geometry of spatial prepositions. *Cognition* 72(2). 167–189.
Geeraerts, Dirk & Hubert Cuyckens. 2007. *The Oxford handbook of cognitive linguistics*. 1st edn. New York, NY: Oxford University Press.
Gentner, Dedre, Brian Bowdle, Phillip Wolff & Consuelo Boronat. 2001. Metaphor is like analogy. In Gentner, Dedre, Holyoak, Keith J. & Kokinov, Boicho N. (ed.), *The analogical mind: Perspectives from cognitive science*, 199–253. Cambridge, MA: MIT Press.
Grady, Joseph. 1997. *Foundations of meaning: Primary metaphors and primary stress*. [Doctoral dissertation, University of California].
Hedblom, Maria M. 2019. *Image schemas and concept invention: Cognitive, logical, and linguistic investigations*. [Doctoral dissertation, University of Magdeburg].
Heritage. The American Heritage Dictionary of the English Language. https://www.ahdictionary.com/word/search.html?q=preposition (23 February, 2023).
Hernández, Patricia. 2012. Est-on aux pizzas comme on est aux casseroles? Sur les emplois métonymiques des syntagmes prépositionnels en à avec un nom d'objet. In *SHS Web of Conferences*, vol. 1, 1759–1776.
Herrmann, J. Berenike. 2013. *Metaphor in academic discourse*. [Doctoral dissertation, Vrije Universiteit].
Holyoak, Keith J. & Dušan Stamenkovic. 2018. Metaphor comprehension: A critical review of theories and evidence. *Psychological Bulletin* 144(6). 641–671.
Kövecses, Zoltán. 2015. *Where metaphors come from: Reconsidering context in metaphor*. New York, NY: Oxford University Press.
Kövecses, Zoltán. 2020. *Extended conceptual metaphor theory*. Cambridge, England: Cambridge University Press.
Krzeszowski, Tomasz P. 1993. The axiological parameter in preconceptional image schemata. In Geiger, Richard A. & Rudzka-Ostyn, Brygida (ed.), *Conceptualizations and mental processing in language*, 307–330. Berlin, Germany: De Gruyter Mouton.
Lakoff, George. 2006. *Whose freedom? The battle over America's most important idea*. New York, NY: Farrar, Straus and Giroux.
Lakoff, George & Mark Johnson. 1980. *Metaphors we live by*. Chicago, IL: The University of Chicago Press.
Langacker, Ronald W. 2008a. The relevance of cognitive grammar for language pedagogy. In Knop, Sabine De & Rycker, Teun De (ed.), *Cognitive approaches to pedagogical grammar*, 7–35. Berlin, Germany: Mouton de Gruyter.
Langacker, Ronald W. 2008b. *Cognitive grammar: A basic introduction*. Oxford, England: Oxford University Press.
Langacker, Ronald W. 2010. Reflections on the functional characterization of spatial prepositions. *Corela* HS-(7). 1–20.
Lapaire, Jean-Rémi. 2017. Grammaire cognitive des prépositions : Épistémologie et applications. *Corela* HS-(22). 1–25.
Lindstromberg, Seth. 2010. *English prepositions explained*. Revised. Amsterdam, The Netherlands: John Benjamins Publishing.
Lu, Wei-Lun & others. 2017. Perspectivization and contextualization in semantic analysis: A parsimonious polysemy approach to in. *Studia Linguistica Universitatis Iagellonicae Cracoviensis* 134(3). 247–264.

Macmillan. Preposition. Macmillan Education. https://www.macmillandictionary.com/dictionary/british/preposition (24 February, 2023).

Merriam-Webster. Merriam-Webster Dictionary Online. https://www.merriam-webster.com/dictionary/preposition (25 February, 2023).

Oxford. Oxford Dictionaries Online. https://www.lexico.com/en/definition/preposition (21 February, 2023).

Quirk, Randolph, Sidney Greenbaum, Geoffrey Leech & Jan Svartvik. 1985. *A comprehensive grammar of the English language*. London, England: Longman.

Radden, Günter & René Dirven. 2007. *Cognitive English grammar*. Vol. 2. Amsterdam, The Netherlands: John Benjamins Publishing.

Sperber, Dan & Deirdre Wilson. 1996. *Relevance: Communication and cognition*. Oxford, England: Blackwell.

Srikumar, Vivek & Dan Roth. 2013. Modeling semantic relations expressed by prepositions. *Transactions of the Association for Computational Linguistics* 1. 231–242.

Sullivan, Karen. 2007. *Grammar in metaphor: A construction grammar account of metaphoric language*. [Doctoral dissertation, University of California].

Szwedek, Aleksander. 2008. Are prepositions metaphorical? In Oleksy, Wiesław & Stalmaszczyk, Piotr (ed.), *Cognitive approaches to language and linguistic data*, 171–180. Frankfurt am Main, Germany: Peter Lang.

Szwedek, Aleksander. 2014. The nature of domains and the relationships between them in metaphorization. *Review of Cognitive Linguistics*. John Benjamins 12(2). 342–374.

Traugott, Elizabeth Closs. 1988. Pragmatic strengthening and grammaticalization. In *Annual Meeting of the Berkeley Linguistics Society*, 406–416. Berkeley, CA: eLanguage. http://linguistics.berkeley.edu/bls/.

Tseng, Min-Yu. 2007. Exploring image schemas as a critical concept: Toward a critical-cognitive linguistic account of image-schematic interactions. *Journal of Literary Semantics* 36(2). 135–157.

Tyler, Andrea & Vyvyan Evans. 2003. *The semantics of English prepositions: Spatial scenes, embodied meaning, and cognition*. Cambridge, England: Cambridge University Press.

Vandeloise, Claude. 2017. The expression of proximity in French and in English. *Corela* HS-(23). 1–23.

Wilson, Deirdre. 2017. Relevance theory. In Huang, Yan (ed.), *The Oxford handbook of pragmatics*, 79–100. Oxford, England: Oxford University Press.

3 Metaphor
Insights from classical and cognitive approaches

3.1 Classical views on metaphor

The roots of the word metaphor are traced back to ancient Greek, and the topic of metaphor has been the subject of ongoing debate since that time. The first debate was whether metaphor is a true or false representation of the world, highlighting the complex relationship between language, meaning, and reality. In Plato's words, it is "an old quarrel between philosophy and poetry" (Republic 607b 5–6), as cited in Steinitz (2015: 33). In his quest for truth, Plato raised concerns about the potential misuse of metaphor for misleading people and diverting them from truth and reality (Aldokhayel 2008: 24). His concerns were primarily driven by allegations made against poets, who were accused of distorting reality and truth through their imitation of the Form (Jannotta 2010: 157).

The debate between truth and metaphor was not limited to poetry. Political discourse also fell under this binary controversy. Politicians were accused of misusing metaphor to manipulate or conceal the truth. However, Aristotle's view on metaphor was primarily academic and detached from the polarized debates of his time. His widely quoted definition of metaphor can be found in his seminal work, *Poetics* (1457b 6–9), which states:

> Metaphor (*metaphora*) consists in giving (*epiphora*) the thing a name (*onomatos*) that belongs to something else, the transference being either from genus to species (*apo tov genous epi eidos*), or from species to genus, or from species to species, or on grounds of analogy.
>
> (Cited in Derrida & Moore 1974: 31)

For Aristotle, the essence of metaphor is transference, which is an accurate translation of the original Greek word *epiphora*. The prefix "meta" signifies "carrying across" from one location to another (Kirby 1997: 532). Transference is achieved through substitution, where a word originally referring to one thing is used to refer to another. In other words, metaphor is merely a substitution of a proper name with a figurative name.

Aristotle's definition of metaphor is built upon three underlying assumptions. First, metaphor operates basically at the level of words. It involves the transference of meaning, specifically focusing on substituting the meanings of individual words rather than entire sentences. Second, transference assumes that the literal meaning of a word represents its original status, while its metaphorical meaning is acquired through the process of substitution. The third principle is the similarity norm, by which transference cannot happen without an analogy between words.

These three assumptions have at least two implications. First, metaphorical language holds a higher status than literal language. This high status is evident in the significant importance that Aristotle attributes to metaphor. Accordingly, metaphor should "elevate one's style and lend an appearance of dignity (*semnos*) to the discourse" (1404b 9), as cited in Moran (1996: 380). Second, metaphor is not equally accessible to all language users. Aristotle emphasizes the significance of this skill by stating that "the greatest thing by far is to be a master of metaphor. It is the one thing that cannot be learnt from others" (1459a 5). Metaphor is a skill reserved for a select few who possess the talent of observing and identifying similarities between seemingly unrelated nouns. In Aristotle's words, metaphor is "a sign of genius, since a good metaphor implies an intuitive perception of the similarity in dissimilars" (1459a 7–8).

Aristotle's view of metaphor may seem uncontroversial. However, his original writings do not clearly explain the mechanism of analogy, leading to the belief that the Aristotelian metaphor involves a cognitive process and that transference is merely the visible and external aspect of metaphor (Driscoll 2012: 28; Travaglini 2015). Other scholars argue that Aristotle did not allude to any cognitive processes, and he views metaphor as a mere skill for talented orators to make their words "impressive and pleasing" (Wood 2015: 135). Away from such controversial and opposing interpretations, Aristotle's focus on the stylistic effects of metaphor confirms its ornamental nature and underscores a lack of any references to its cognitive aspect.

Aristotle is recognized as the first scholar to define metaphor and conduct "extensive philosophical treatment that allowed researchers' interest in a metaphor to survive through the centuries" (Deibler 1989: 12). His seminal theory has served as a solid foundation for Western schools of thought, whether in his definition of metaphor or his endorsement of its rhetorical efficacy.

Aristotle's views of metaphor in public speaking were highly regarded and widely adopted in the education of orators during the Roman era. Notable Roman thinkers, including Cicero and Quintilian, emphasized the importance of mastering metaphor in order to create aesthetically pleasing and impressive speeches. For example, Cicero, in his work *De Oratore, III, 37*, likened the use of metaphor in a speech to the adornment of an outfit:

> Metaphor was judged by its effect on the hearer in the way that clothes impress the viewer. The effect of the former is the pleasure of the orator's

eloquence is the same as the pleasure of the noble's elegance by virtue of his or her clothes.

(Cited in Digonnet 2014: 47)

During the Medieval period, metaphor flourished within the field of *The Scriptures* studies. Saint Augustine, a renowned medieval theologian (354–430), strongly advocated "teaching rhetoric in Christian education" (Moreno 2008: 31). This emphasis on rhetoric led to the widespread use of metaphor in sermons as a stylistic device, enabling preachers to convey the nature of God and emphasize His truths with greater clarity and impact. St. Thomas Aquinas (1225–1274) carried on the tradition of utilizing metaphor and rhetoric in Christian education. He also made significant contributions by compiling a separate work on secular metaphors.

Both religious and secular metaphors were widely used until the Age of Enlightenment. This era, however, was marked not only by a flourishing religious discourse but also by the growth of poetry. As a result, the use of metaphor became a subject of debate and confusion, as it oscillated between the divine perspective as represented in *The Scriptures* and the human perspective as embodied in poetry. From the theologians' point of view, their metaphors were considered divine as they were about God's absolute truths, whereas poetic metaphors were not highly valued as they were accused of diverting people from these essential truths.

Poetry was flourishing not only in Rome but also in neighboring regions. During the 11th and 12th centuries, Arab poets elevated the use of metaphor as a hallmark of exceptional talent, a trend supported by the renowned guidebook *Kitābu albadī'i* (*The Book of Ornate Style*) written by Ibn al-Mu'tazz in 908. The title of this book succinctly encapsulates its focus. During the same period, Abd alQāhir al-Jurjānī wrote another foundational book entitled *Asrār al-Balāghah* (*The Secrets of Eloquence*). In this book, Al-Jurjānī (1991: 30) provided the following definition of metaphor:

> In a sentence, metaphor occurs when a word has a basic meaning in the linguistic system, as evidenced by testimonies that this meaning is unique to this word. Then, a poet, or anyone who is not a poet, uses this specific word in a sense that contrasts with its basic meaning and thus transfers that word to the new meaning, but in a non-engaging way. As a result, in the new context, that particular word appears to be a loan.
>
> (Translated by the author)

In this same book, al-Jurjānī highlights the captivating impact of expertly crafted metaphors, evoking a "poetic thrill" and showcasing "the existence of talent and skill" (Al-Jurjānī 1991: 113). In his examination of the disparities between metaphor and simile, al-Jurjānī asserts that metaphors require a greater cognitive effort, as the source domain is comprehended even when signal words are not explicitly stated. In general, al-Jurjānī's approach was original, offering a framework for the "identification, classification, and analysis of simile and metaphor" (Geraghy 2013: 3).

Although it still represents a reference book for modern Arab literary criticism, al-Jurjānī's work is still within the realm of the beauty of poetic imagery and the secrets of eloquence, as its title says. In the same vein, Ibn Ezra, in his famous book *Kitāb al-Muḥāḍarah wa-al-Mudhākarah*, combined the rich heritage of Arab rhetoric with the classical traditions of ancient Hebrew and Greek cultures, applying them to the interpretation of *The Hebrew Scriptures*. As cited in Cohen (2000: 4), Ibn Ezra defines metaphor as "borrowing a word for something not known using something already known" (Ibn Ezra 1975: 120). This meaning is encapsulated in the Arabic word *istiara*, meaning "borrowing".

The concept of metaphor was widely regarded either as a transference of meaning, as in the Aristotelian tradition, or as a borrowing of words, as in Arabian literary traditions. Regardless of the terminology used, metaphor was limited to the realm of language and used solely to enhance the beauty and power of eloquence. This narrow perspective persisted until the Age of Enlightenment.

During the Enlightenment, philosophers sought to understand the role of language in conveying knowledge, leading to a contentious debate around a dichotomy between reason (ratio) and eloquence (oratio). This debate revolved around whether scholars should employ literal or figurative language when studying empirical reality. Generally, there was a prevailing inclination towards the latter rather than the former. Literal words were valued for clarity and precision, while metaphors were discouraged for ambiguity and elusiveness. Influential philosopher, Thomas Hobbes, went so far as to declare that scientific truths must only be communicated through literal words and that metaphors were as worthless as any "senseless and ambiguous words", as cited in Petrica (2011: 33). He even included metaphors among "the seven causes of absurdity", as cited in Lambourn (2001: 38). Like Hobbes, John Locke warned against the use of metaphors, referring to them as perfect cheats. He believed that metaphors were frequently employed in "discourses that pretend to inform or instruct", leading to potential misunderstandings and confusion (Cohen 1978: 4).

The anti-metaphor stance of the Enlightenment era was challenged by 19th-century philosophers, who began to explore the relationship between language, thought, and reality from a different perspective. Immanuel Kant, for example, considered language's clarity and precision an essential element of pure reason. His work on the concept of schema marked a crucial breakthrough in comprehending metaphors and the "way of relating percepts to concepts" (Oakley 2010: 215). Accordingly, a particular schema links a concept to its referent and bridges "the gap between the formal and the material aspects of cognition", as cited in Hampe and Grady (2005: 17).

Kant's concept of schema marked a departure from the ornate style associated with the classical view of metaphor and emphasized imagination instead of the mechanical word substitution. Today, Kant's contribution continues to be highly regarded for its "recognition of imagination as the locus of human meaning, thought, and judgment" (Hampe & Grady 2005: 17). Similarly, Jäkel (1999) devoted an entire article giving credit to Kant's forgotten contributions to the theory of cognitive metaphor.

During the 19th century, other philosophers, such as Giambattista Vico, Johann Wolfgang von Goethe, and Jean-Paul Sartre, also made significant contributions to metaphor studies, moving away from a binary approach to language that viewed it solely in terms of literal and metaphorical dichotomies. Their work was extended by Gustav Gerber, Alfred Biese, and Friedrich Nietzsche (Nerlich & Clarke 2001). In his essay *Truth and Lie in an Extra-Moral Sense*, Nietzsche was profoundly critical of the duality between the literal and metaphorical interpretations of language. He also warned about the dangers of adhering too closely to particular truths because:

> Truths are illusions which we have forgotten are illusions; they are metaphors that have become worn out and have been drained of sensuous force, coins which have lost their embossing and are now considered as metal and no longer as coins.
>
> (Kaufmann 1954: 47)

The philosophical debate about the nature of metaphor and its relationship to truth came to an end during the first half of the 20th century. In 1936, Richards published his influential work, *The Philosophy of Rhetoric*, which established the framework for the interaction theory of metaphor and marked the end of the positivist approach to metaphor (Deibler 1989). The interaction theory of metaphor posits that metaphor arises from an interaction between the meaning of "two thoughts of different things active together and supported by a single word, or phrase" Richards (1936: 93), as cited by Goodblatt and Glicksohn (2017: 5). Contrary to the substitution theory of metaphor, Richards (1936: 94) defines metaphor as "a borrowing between and intercourse of *thoughts*, a transaction between contexts", as cited in Luporini (2013: 22).

The notion of interaction was further developed by Max Black in the 1960s, building on the foundation laid by Richards. Black clearly described his analysis of metaphor as "an *interactive* view of metaphor" (Black 1955: 285). In his well-known example, "Man is a wolf", Black explains his view of metaphor as follows: the two subjects in this statement are "man" as the principal subject and "wolf" as the subsidiary one. To understand this statement as a metaphor, you must first understand "wolf" through its related meanings and implications. Metaphor works by applying the meanings and implications of the subsidiary subject to the principal one.

In Black's words, to call a man a wolf is "to evoke the wolf-system of related commonplaces" (Black 1955: 288).

Black's contribution to metaphor studies is significant in two main ways. First, he was the first to suggest that metaphor belongs to semantics and pragmatics rather than an ornate style or quest for knowledge and its truths. Second, Black made several references to the conceptual dimensions of metaphor. For example, he described metaphor as "a distinctive *intellectual* operation" (Black 1955: 293). He also affirmed that a literal paraphrasing of a metaphor causes "a loss in *cognitive* content" (Black 1955: 293). Interestingly, both terms "intellectual" and "cognitive" are emphasized in the original texts, which entail an awareness that metaphor involves conceptual dimensions rather than a mere mechanical substitution or comparison. Despite these recurrent references to cognitive aspects of metaphor, Back could not earn any recognition from modern cognitive linguists. For some critics, Black's theory of metaphor is about "the process of metaphor comprehension" (Goodblatt & Glicksohn 2017: 3) rather than the nature of metaphor itself. Lakoff acknowledges that he has read Black's work but has disavowed any connection between his conceptual metaphor theory (henceforth CMT) and Black's interactionist theory. He replied, "I had read Black and I had no interest in what Black was doing" (Pires de Oliveira 2001: 24).

In addition to Black's contribution, Ricœur's views have been very significant. In contrast to Aristotelian theory, Ricœur (1978: 145) contended that metaphor belongs to semantics and, as such, must be studied at the sentence level rather than the word level:

> The semantic point of view and the rhetorical point of view begin to differentiate only when the metaphor is placed in the context of the sentence and treated as a case no longer of a deviant denomination but impertinent predication.
>
> (Ricœur 1975: 8)

In his renowned work, *La Métaphore Vive*, Ricœur clarified that metaphor is based on semantic innovation, "thanks to which a new pertinence, a new congruence, is established in such a way that the utterance 'makes sense' as a whole" (Ricœur 1978: 146). This new congruence is rooted in the idea of semantic proximity, which involves a "move or shift in the logical distance, from the far to the near" (Ricœur 1978: 147). In this shift, imagination resolves the semantic tension between incongruent concepts, allowing us "to see the *like* is to see the same in spite of, and through, the different" (Ricœur 1978: 148). He also affirmed that imagination "contributes concretely to the epochè of ordinary reference and to the projection of new possibilities of re-describing the world" (Ricœur 1978: 154). This process of redescribing the world through metaphor involves a kind of "split reference" (Ricœur 1978: 153), reminiscent of the Majorca storytellers' expression: "it was and it was not".

Throughout his 1978 article, Ricœur repeatedly refers to the cognitive aspect of metaphor, as indicated by the use of the term "cognition" in the article's title and the term "cognitive" on ten separate occasions throughout the 18-page text. While his ideas of the "cognitive import", "cognitive structure", or "cognitive process" are not fully developed, they are nevertheless linked to his explanation of "the impertinent predication" and the role of metaphor as "the prompt to think more" (Cazeaux 2011: 3). Nonetheless, his recognition of the importance of the cognitive aspect of metaphor has provided a useful framework for further research into the nature of metaphor and its role in human cognition.

In 1979, only one year after Ricœur's article, the first edition of Ortony's *Metaphor and Thought* was published. This book featured a famous chapter by Michael Reddy entitled "The Conduit Metaphor". The following year, *Metaphors We Live By* was published, which is considered a seminal book that marked the beginning of the cognitive perspective on metaphor.

3.2 Cognitive view on metaphor

In order to understand metaphor from a cognitive perspective, it is essential to review the main principles of cognitive linguistics. According to Geeraerts and Cuyckens (2007a: 5), cognitive linguistics is "the study of language in its cognitive function". This definition is based on the idea that linguistic structures reflect conceptual structures and that language is an inseparable part of the human cognitive system. In other words, language is not independent of general cognition but "uses general cognitive mechanisms" (Lakoff 1982: 4).

Cognitive linguistics originated in the early 1970s as a response to the prevailing Chomskyan generative grammar (Evans & Green 2006: 3; Gibbs 2006: 42). The generative approach was criticized for overemphasizing formal rules and structures in generating and interpreting language while disregarding its semantic dimensions. In contrast, cognitive linguistics embraces "the belief that linguistic knowledge involves not just knowledge of the language, but knowledge of the world as mediated by the language" (Geeraerts & Cuyckens 2007a: 7).

In 1980, George Lakoff and Mark Johnson published their influential book *Metaphors We Live By*, which marked a significant turning point in metaphor studies. This book introduced an original approach to understanding metaphor, which would come to be known as "conceptual metaphor theory". Its main principle is that "metaphor is pervasive in everyday life, not just in language but in thought and action. Our ordinary conceptual system, in terms of which we both think and act, is fundamentally metaphorical in nature" (Lakoff & Johnson 1980: 3). Contrary to traditional theories that view metaphor as primarily a linguistic phenomenon, Lakoff and Johnson (1999: 118) argue that metaphor is basically "conceptual and everyday thought is largely metaphorical".

The cognitive perspective suggests that we should not rely solely on linguistic tools to understand and explain metaphors but instead look for their underlying conceptual principles. At this underlying level, a conceptual metaphor relies primarily on correspondence or mapping between a source domain and a target domain. A conceptual metaphor is defined as "a systematic set of correspondences between two domains of experience" (Kövecses 2020: 2). Various expressions are coined to describe this mapping, such as "cross-domain mapping", "two-domain mapping", "structure-mapping", "analogical mapping", and "conceptual projection" (Geeraerts 1997; Gentner et al. 2001; Lakoff 1988; Radden & Dirven 2007).

Despite the ongoing theoretical debate on the nature of conceptual mapping, two fundamental principles define how correspondences are established: unidirectionality and invariance. Unidirectionality specifies that the direction of metaphorical mapping between the two domains matters. The "natural direction", according to Kövecses (2010: 329), begins from the concrete and finishes at the abstract and not vice versa. The reasoning behind this principle lies in the fact that "target domains tend to be more vague and incomplete than source domains" (Gibbs 1996: 311). In addition to the principle of unidirectionality, the correspondences between conceptual domains are also governed by the invariance hypothesis, which aims to maintain the integrity of the image-schematic structure and the semantic properties of the target domain. This hypothesis ensures that the metaphorical mapping does not distort the essential properties of the target domain. As Turner (1990: 252) affirms, "we are constrained not to violate whatever image-schematic structure may be possessed by non-image components of the target". This means that when we use a metaphor to understand an abstract concept in terms of a concrete one, we need to ensure that the essential structure and features of the abstract concept are not lost or distorted in the process. By following the invariance hypothesis, we can maintain the coherence and consistency of the metaphorical mapping between the two domains and avoid confusing or misleading interpretations.

Metaphors are so prevalent in language that they are often considered unquestionable, natural, and unconsciously produced and processed. These commonplace metaphors are known as "conventional" and become "part of larger systematic metaphors which also have very noticeable 'live' metaphorical extensions" (Geeraerts & Cuyckens 2007b: 32). Over time, through repeated use, conventionalized metaphors become familiar and may lose some of their metaphorical meaning. As a result, we may use these metaphors "without apparently noticing their metaphorical basis" (Gentner et al. 2001: 211). Conventionalization can lead to a state where the once metaphorical meaning is understood as literal and included in one of the entries in a dictionary (Holyoak & Stamenkovic 2018: 644).

Conventionalization is not limited to metaphorical expressions; their underlying conceptual metaphors can become "entrenched ways of thinking about or understanding abstract domains" (Kövecses 2010: 34) or "conventionalized systems of reasoning", as Gentner et al. (2001: 241) argue. Seen from another perspective, metaphors can be viewed on a continuum of sleeping/waking distinction based on "different degrees of metaphor activation" (Müller 2009; Müller & Tag 2010: 85). According to this dynamic view, the waking metaphors are highly activated, while the sleeping ones are subjected to a lower activation. This means that the use of metaphors is the outcome of dynamic cognitive activation and salience influenced by context and discourse dynamics.

In the actual production of discourse, we usually mix metaphors from widely divergent source domains. For example, Shen and Balaban (1999) argue that metaphor coherence depends on whether the discourse is planned or unplanned. They assert that "special planning seems to be required to make discourse metaphorically coherent" (Shen & Balaban 1999: 151), while metaphors in unplanned discourse appear "more like free, uncontrolled 'navigation' between a large number of root metaphors than a consistent elaboration of any unifying root metaphors" (Shen & Balaban 1999: 151). In the same vein, Kimmel (2010) examines metaphor coherence in a corpus extracted from the British newspapers *Sun* and *Guardian*, and he concludes that "journalists combine metaphors into complex, yet well-formed arguments on a regular basis" (Kimmel 2010: 97). In his extended view of CMT, Kövecses (2020) explains that target domains, which evoke the topic in a given discourse, usually have various aspects that require various source domains. As a result, seemingly incompatible linguistic metaphors can be mixed even within a single clause. In metaphor comprehension, these incompatibilities are not activated at the lowest level of the schematicity hierarchy (Kövecses 2020: 133).

In addition to metaphor, metonymy is "a ubiquitous feature of everyday speech" (Gibbs 1994: 12), and they both "constitute basic schemes by which people conceptualize their experience and the external world" (Gibbs 1994: 1). However, metaphor and metonymy differ in mapping. "While metaphor involves mapping between domains, metonymy is an intra-domain phenomenon", Deignan (2005: 73) wrote. In Lakoff's words, metonymy is "a part (a subcategory or member or sub-model) that stands for the whole category" (Lakoff 1987: 79). There are several types of metonymic models that people use to conceptualize their experience of the world. They include A PART FOR THE WHOLE, A PRODUCT FOR THE PRODUCER, A PLACE FOR THE INSTITUTION, AN INSTITUTION FOR THE PEOPLE RESPONSIBLE, and AN OBJECT USED FOR THE USER.

It is important to note that scholars have different views regarding the relationship between metaphor and metonymy. While Deignan emphasizes the differences between these two concepts, other scholars such as Kövecses, Radden, and Barcelona argue that metonymy and metaphor share a similar cognitive structure and mapping type. More specifically, Kövecses (2010: 173) defines metonymy as "a cognitive process in which one conceptual entity, the vehicle, provides mental access to another conceptual entity, the target, within the same domain or idealized cognitive model (ICM)". Along the same lines, metonymy is defined by Barcelona (2003: 32–33) as "the conceptual mapping of a cognitive domain onto another domain, both domains being included in the same domain, or ICM so that the source provides mental access to the target". On the other hand, Steen et al. (2010) distinguish between metaphor and metonymy in terms of a contrast between basic and contextual meaning. They suggest that metonymy arises "where two senses may be contrasted but where the contrast is bridged by contiguity instead of similarity". This comparison between metonymy and metaphor entails understanding an abstract concept *via* a concrete concept in a metonymy, while metaphor consists of understanding an abstract concept *as* a concrete concept.

Metaphors and metonymies are not just conceptually based. They are also "context-induced" (Kövecses 2020: 11). Thus, it is important to consider the role of context in which these mappings emerge. Initially, this context includes the universal aspects of the human body. Accordingly, conceptual metaphors arise from an embodied mind grounded in the human body and experience (Johnson & Lakoff 2002; Lakoff 1982). The embodiment principle assumes that source-to-target mapping is "grounded in physical and cultural experience" (Lakoff & Johnson 1980: 197). This principle has been broadened to encompass additional contextual factors beyond the human body, with a focus on the interaction between the body and the various aspects of the environment. For example, Rohrer (2007: 344) asserts that embodiment is not restricted to the physical body but encompasses "the body in space, the body as interacts with the physical and social environment".

More recently, metaphor studies have started to explore the wider context in which metaphors are generated. For example, Kövecses (2015) has devoted an entire book to exploring the context in which metaphors emerge. Additionally, he proposed a comprehensive perspective on the role of context in metaphor within his extended view of CMT. He identified four types of contexts: situational, discourse, conceptual-cognitive, and bodily. Each type includes several factors. The situational context includes physical, social, and cultural situations. The discourse context includes the surrounding discourse, previous discourse knowledge about the speaker, the topic, the hearer, and the dominant forms of discourse. The conceptual-cognitive context involves our metaphorical conceptual system, the prevalent ideology, history, and common concerns and interests. Finally, the fourth type of context includes correlations in experience, bodily conditions, and body specificities (Kövecses 2020).

The role of context implies that the human mind is embedded in concrete contexts while simultaneously possessing the ability to engage in abstract thinking and reasoning. To address this paradox, Johnson (1987) proposed that the embodied mind prompts abstract image schemas within our conceptual system. "When we understand something as having an abstract structure, we understand that structure in terms of image schemas" (Lakoff 1987: 283). An image schema is defined by Johnson (1987: xiv) as "a recurring, dynamic pattern of our perceptual interactions and motor programs that gives coherence and structure to our experience". For Oakley (2010: 214), an image schema is "a condensed redescription of perceptual experience for the purpose of mapping spatial structure onto conceptual structure". Hampe (2005: 2) has compiled an exhaustive list of 30 types of image schemas. However, for the sake of brevity, the five most common schemas are as follows:

- Container: the image of an object capable of holding other objects.
- Source-path-goal: the image of a path between a starting and an endpoint.
- Center-periphery: the image of a central point with surrounding areas of lesser importance.
- Balance: the image of a stable equilibrium between two opposing forces or elements.
- Part-whole: the image of a larger entity composed of smaller constituent parts.

These image schemas are not fixed mental representations but rather dynamic, fluid patterns that can be combined and modified to form more complex structures. For example, the SOURCE-PATH-GOAL image schema can be used to reason about the logical structure of an argument or a narrative. In contrast, the PART-WHOLE schema can be used to reason about the structure of a complex system or organization.

While image schemas can provide explanations for certain aspects of conceptual mapping, the question remains about how contextual factors and cognitive operations are interconnected. Kövecses (2020) suggests that metaphors are formulated in a discourse situation in which contextual factors are present and active in the working memory. When a contextual meaning is triggered and expressed at the mental space level, the conceptualizer is primed to create a conceptual pathway connecting the contextual meaning to an image schematic metaphor. Then this same "pathway is completed through the specification of the image-schema metaphor at the frame- and domain-levels", as Kövecses (2020: 166) explains. This process is built on the premise that metaphor consists of interconnected levels of schematic hierarchy ranging from the most schematic, the image schema level, through the domain level, then the frame level, and ending at the least schematic level, the mental space. These four levels constitute the multilevel view of metaphor and the core of Kövecses's extended theory.

Metaphor will continue to attract scholars across various disciplines in order to comprehend its multifaceted nature. New insights from psychology, cognitive science, and related disciplines will help us understand how we produce and process metaphors in real discourse situations. These issues can become particularly intricate when adept language users, such as politicians, master the art (or science) of metaphor.

References

Aldokhayel, Reyadh S. 2008. *The event structure metaphor: The case of Arabic*. [Doctoral dissertation, Ball State University].
Barcelona, Antonio. 2003. On the plausibility of claiming a metonymic motivation for conceptual metaphor. In Barcelona, Antonio (ed.), *Metaphor and metonymy at the crossroads: A cognitive perspective*, 31–58. Berlin, Germany: Mouton de Gruyter.
Black, Max. 1955. Metaphor. *Proceedings of the Aristotelian Society* 55(1). 273–294.
Cazeaux, Clive. 2011. Living metaphor. *Studi Filosofici* 34. 291–308.
Cohen, Mordechai. 2000. Moses Ibn Ezra vs. Maimonides: Argument for a poetic definition of metaphor (Isti, ara). *Journal of Middle Eastern Literatures* 11. 1–28.
Cohen, Ted. 1978. Metaphor and the cultivation of intimacy. *Critical Inquiry* 5(1). 3–12.
Deibler, Timothy Alan. 1989. *A philosophical semantic intentionality theory of metaphor*. [Doctoral dissertation, Rice University].
Deignan, Alice. 2005. A corpus linguistic perspective on the relationship between metonymy and metaphor. *Style*. Northern Illinois University 39(1). 72–91.
Derrida, Jacques & FCT Moore. 1974. White mythology: Metaphor in the text of philosophy. *New Literary History*. JSTOR 6(1). 5–74.
Digonnet, Rémi. 2014. Power and metaphor. Towards more executive power in American presidents' inaugural addresses. *Lexis* 8. 45–65.
Driscoll, Sean. 2012. Aristotle's a priori metaphor. *Aporia* 22(1). 20–31.
Evans, Vyvyan & Melanie Green. 2006. *Cognitive linguistics: An introduction*. 1st edn. Edinburgh, Scotland: Edinburgh University Press.
Geeraerts, Dirk. 1997. Diachronic prototype semantics. In Geeraerts, Dirk (ed.), *A contribution to historical lexicology*, 8–52. Oxford, England: Clarendon Press.
Geeraerts, Dirk & Hubert Cuyckens. 2007a. Introducing cognitive linguistics. In Geeraerts, Dirk & Cuyckens, Hubert (ed.), *The Oxford handbook of cognitive linguistics*. Oxford, England/New York, NY: Oxford University Press.
Geeraerts, Dirk & Hubert Cuyckens. 2007b. *The Oxford handbook of cognitive linguistics*. 1st edn. New York, NY: Oxford University Press.
Gentner, Dedre, Brian Bowdle, Phillip Wolff & Consuelo Boronat. 2001. Metaphor is like analogy. In Gentner, Dedre, Holyoak, Keith J. & Kokinov, Boicho N. (ed.), *The analogical mind: Perspectives from cognitive science*, 199–253. Cambridge, MA: MIT Press.
Geraghy, Sean D. 2013. *Classically modern: ʿAbd al-Qāhir al-Jurjānī's theory of metaphor in the interpretation of contemporary Arabic fiction*. [Doctoral dissertation, University of Wisconsin-Madison].
Gibbs, Raymond W. 1994. *The poetics of mind: Figurative thought, language, and understanding*. 1st edn. Cambridge, England: Cambridge University Press.
Gibbs, Raymond W. 1996. Why many concepts are metaphorical. *Cognition*. Elsevier 61(3). 309–319.
Gibbs, Raymond W. 2006. Cognitive linguistics and metaphor research: Past successes, skeptical questions, future challenges. *Documentação de Estudos em Lingüística Teórica e Aplicada* 22(SPE). 1–20.
Goodblatt, Chanita & Joseph Glicksohn. 2017. Bidirectionality and metaphor: An introduction. *Poetics Today* 38(1). 1–14.
Hampe, Beate. 2005. Image schemas in cognitive linguistics: Introduction. In Grady, Joseph E. & Hampe, Beate (ed.), *From perception to meaning: Image schemas in cognitive linguistics*, 1–13. Berlin, Germany: Walter de Gruyter.

Metaphor: insights from classical and cognitive approaches 33

Hampe, Beate & Joseph E. Grady. 2005. *From perception to meaning: Image schemas in cognitive linguistics.* 1st edn. Berlin, Germany: Walter de Gruyter.

Holyoak, Keith J. & Dušan Stamenkovic. 2018. Metaphor comprehension: A critical review of theories and evidence. *Psychological Bulletin* 144(6). 641–671.

Ibn Ezra, Moses. 1975. *Kitāb al-Muḥāḍarah wa-al-Mudhākarah.* (Ed.) Halkin, Abraham Solomon. Mekize Nirdamim.

Jäkel, Olaf. 1999. Kant, Blumenberg, Weinrich: Some forgotten contributions to the cognitive theory of metaphor. *Amsterdam Studies in the Theory and History of Linguistic Science Series.* JOHN BENJAMINS BV 4(4). 9–28.

Jannotta, Anthony. 2010. Plato's theory of forms: analogy and metaphor in Plato's republic. *Undergraduate Review* 6(1). 154–157.

Johnson, Mark. 1987. *The body in the mind: The bodily basis of meaning, imagination and reason.* London, England/ Chicago, IL: The University of Chicago Press.

Johnson, Mark & George Lakoff. 2002. Why cognitive linguistics requires embodied realism. *Cognitive Linguistics* 13(3). 245–264.

Al-Jurjānī, ᶜAbd Al-Qāhir. 1991. *Asrār al-Balāghah [The Mysteries of Eloquence].* Jeddah, KSA: Dar Al- Madani.

Kaufmann, Walter. 1954. *The Portable Nietzsche.* New York: The Viking Press.

Kimmel, Michael. 2010. Why we mix metaphors (and mix them well): Discourse coherence, conceptual metaphor, and beyond. *Journal of Pragmatics.* Elsevier 42(1). 97–115.

Kirby, John. 1997. Aristotle on metaphor. *American Journal of Philology* 118(4). 517–554.

Kövecses, Zoltán. 2010. *Metaphor: A practical introduction.* 2nd edn. Oxford, England: Oxford University Press.

Kövecses, Zoltán. 2015. *Where metaphors come from: Reconsidering context in metaphor.* New York, NY: Oxford University Press.

Kövecses, Zoltán. 2020. *Extended conceptual metaphor theory.* Cambridge, England: Cambridge University Press.

Lakoff, George. 1982. Categories: An essay in cognitive linguistics. In Yang, In-Seok (ed.), *Linguistics in the morning calm*, 139–193. Seoul, South Korea: Hanshin.

Lakoff, George. 1987. *Women, fire, and dangerous things.* Chicago, IL: The University of Chicago Press.

Lakoff, George. 1988. Cognitive semantics. In Eco, Umberto (ed.), *Meaning and mental representations*, 119–154. Bloomington, CA: Indiana University Press.

Lakoff, George & Mark Johnson. 1980. *Metaphors we live by.* Chicago, IL: The University of Chicago Press.

Lakoff, George & Mark Johnson. 1999. *Philosophy in the flesh: The embodied mind and its challenges to Western thought.* New York, NY: Basic books.

Lambourn, David Malcolm. 2001. *Metaphor in social thought.* [Doctoral dissertation, University of Warwick].

Luporini, Antonella. 2013. *Metaphor in times of crisis: Metaphorical representations of the global crisis in The Financial Times and Il Sole 24 Ore 2008.* [Doctoral dissertation, Università Di Pisa].

Moran, Richard. 1996. Artifice and persuasion: The work of metaphor in the rhetoric. In Rorty, Amelie Oksenberg (ed.), *Essays on Aristotle's Rhetoric*, 385–398. Berkeley, CA: University of California Press.

Moreno, Marco Aponte. 2008. *Metaphors in Hugo Chávez's political discourse: Conceptualizing nation, revolution, and opposition.* [Doctoral dissertation, The City University of New York].

Müller, Cornelia. 2009. *Metaphors dead and alive, sleeping and waking: A dynamic view*. Chicago, IL: University of Chicago Press.
Müller, Cornelia & Susanne Tag. 2010. The dynamics of metaphor: Foregrounding and activating metaphoricity in conversational interaction. *Cognitive Semiotics*. De Gruyter 6(Supplement). 85–120.
Nerlich, Brigitte & David Clarke. 2001. Mind, meaning and metaphor: The philosophy and psychology of metaphor in 19th-century Germany. *History of the Human Sciences* 14(2). 39–62.
Oakley, Todd. 2010. Image schemas. In Geeraerts, Dirk & Cuyckens, Hubert (ed.), *The Oxford handbook of cognitive linguistics*, 214–235. Oxford, England: Oxford University Press.
Petrica, Monica. 2011. *Cognitive metaphors in political discourse in Malta and the case of EU-membership debate*. [Doctoral dissertation, Ludwig-Maximilians-Universität].
Pires de Oliveira, Roberta. 2001. Language and ideology: An interview with George Lakoff. In Dirven, René, Hawkins, Bruce & Sandikcioglu, Esra (ed.), *Language and ideology volume 1: Theoretical cognitive approaches*, 23–47. Amsterdam, The Netherlands: John Benjamins Publishing.
Radden, Günter & René Dirven. 2007. *Cognitive English grammar*. Vol. 2. Amsterdam, The Netherlands: John Benjamins Publishing.
Richards, Ivor Armstrong. 1936. *The philosophy of rhetoric*. London: Oxford University Press.
Ricœur, Paul. 1975. *La métaphore vive*. Paris, France: Editons du Seuil.
Ricœur, Paul. 1978. The metaphorical process as cognition, imagination, and feeling. *Critical Inquiry*. JSTOR 5(1). 143–159.
Rohrer, Tim. 2007. The body in space: Dimensions of embodiment. *Body, Language and Mind* 1. 339–378.
Shen, Yeshayahu & Noga Balaban. 1999. Metaphorical (in) coherence in discourse. *Discourse Processes*. Taylor & Francis 28(2). 139–153.
Steen, Gerard J., Aletta G. Dorst, J. Berenike Herrmann, Anna Kaal, Tina Krennmayr & Trijntje Pasma. 2010. *A method for linguistic metaphor identification: From MIP to MIPVU*. Amsterdam, The Netherlands: John Benjamins Publishing.
Steinitz, Joseph. 2015. *What's metaphor got to do with it? Troping and counter-troping in holocaust victim language*. [Doctoral dissertation, University of Iowa].
Travaglini, Graziella. 2015. Aristotle's mimesis metaphorike: Between semantic universality and ontological determinateness. *Rivista Italiana di Filosofia del Linguaggio* 9(2). 58–73.
Turner, Mark. 1990. Aspects of the invariance hypothesis. *Cognitive Linguistics* 1(2). 247–255.
Wood, Matthew Stephen. 2015. *Aristotle and the question of metaphor*. [Doctoral dissertation, University of Ottawa].

4 The power of prepositions in political discourse

4.1 Political language

The language of politics consists of "a wide and diverse set of discourses, or genres, or registers that can be classified as forms of political language", as Bayley (2005: 3) notes. These various forms of political language, whether spoken or written, are produced by a range of institutions, such as government, parliament, political parties, interest groups, the media, and administrative bodies. Consequently, there are various terms to describe the use of language in political contexts, such as the language of politics, political language, political discourse, political text, political communication, and political rhetoric. These terminological variations reflect the long-standing effort to understand the relationship between language and politics that has been ongoing for centuries.

The definition of political discourse is closely tied to the definition of politics itself. Politics typically refers to the activities associated with governing a nation or community. These activities, which involve the enactment of laws that affect citizens, require that politicians seek the consent of these citizens through democratic means such as elections and representation. In this process, the interests of citizens are reconciled and given equal consideration. In order to achieve this conciliation, negotiation plays a crucial role, wherein information, ideas, emotions, values, and attitudes are freely expressed and exchanged. Within this frame, politics refers to "the institutionalized and noninstitutionalized *arenas of power relations* wherein collectivities *negotiate* the distribution and redistribution of material and symbolic resources", as Gronbeck (2004: 147) notes. Negotiation entails employing language to express, reconcile, or regulate conflicting interests. The potency of language becomes evident as it prevents these conflicting factions from escalating their disputes into full-blown wars and contributes to the preservation of stability and order.

From an alternative perspective, politics pertains to the activities of various actors engaged in deliberation before passing laws that promote the common good. It is "most fundamentally about making choices about how to act in response to circumstances and goals, it is about choosing *policies*", according to Fairclough and Fairclough (2012: 1). The decision-making process is built on the ideal of the rule of free men by free men engaging in deliberation and requires careful and wise of language to prevent hasty decisions and one-sided arguments. The power of language in deliberative politics is manifest in its ability to facilitate comprehension and interpretation of ideas.

In its negotiation and deliberation dimensions, political language employs various strategies to shape public opinion, persuade voters, and "channel political thought and action in certain directions" (Connolly 1993: 1). In addition to rhetorical devices, politicians often use framing techniques and loaded language. These strategies and techniques can be used in ethical and transparent communication, but they can also be utilized in manipulative or deceptive ways.

As Jucker (1997: 123) explains, "politicians use language not only to persuade but also to inform, to entertain, and perhaps also to deceive or cover up". The misuse of language exploits its power for manipulation and propaganda, often observed in undemocratic regimes that lack or limit the practices of negotiation and deliberation. The power of language can also be exploited in a subtle manner through sophisticated discursive practices that aim to manufacture "political consent" (Herman & Chomsky 1988; Ringmar 2007).

The recognition of the power of language in politics is not a recent revelation. In ancient Greece, political discourse revolved around this same topic. The following section explores the historical evolution of the language's role in politics.

4.2   The history of political discourse analysis

The study of political language finds its origins in the work of Ancient Greek scholars who examined political discourse within the realm of rhetoric, striving to foster virtuous and ethical politics. In Greek mythology, rhetoric was associated with persuasive techniques and magic impact. Peitho, the goddess of persuasion, seduction, and charming speech, further underscores the inclination to employ language for manipulation and seduction. In academia, and away from myths and magic, Plato urged politicians to use language properly to ensure an "antirhetorical, truth-oriented politics" (Gronbeck 2004: 137). Accordingly, political values should be grounded in reason-based truths (episteme) rather than emotions and popular discourses.

Plato's views should be interpreted within the context of an academic debate on the most effective means of persuasion. The sophists were interested in the art of persuasion and preoccupied with using persuasion techniques to teach moral virtues and excellence to young political leaders. The tension between the Platonian dialectician and the Sophist rhetorician centered on the use of language in politics. It raised important questions about what constituted philosophical or rhetorical truth and whether language should appeal to reason or emotion.

Aristotle is credited with resolving the conflict between Plato and the Sophists by arguing that rhetoric can be a valuable tool as long as it complements reason and aligns with the accepted values and convictions of the public. He defined rhetoric as "an ability, in each [particular] case, to see the available means of persuasion" (Jamar 2001: 62). He also referred to it as "the art and practice of coming to sound judgment". These definitions highlight that rhetoric is not just about persuading others but also about discovering the most effective means of persuasion in a given situation.

The power of language lies in its capacity to formulate arguments that resonate with the audience, operating through three modes of persuasion. In Aristotle's terms, these modes are called *Logos*, *Ethos*, and *Pathos*. Accordingly, a skilled rhetorician knows how to activate the right appeal at the right time and with the right audience. The first appeal, Logos, is concerned with logical reasoning and entails "setting up a line of reasoning with constellations of claims and supporting arguments" (Hornikx 2005: 9). Ethos, the second rhetorical appeal, emphasizes the speaker's positive qualities and character, thereby fostering trust and credibility among the audience towards the conveyed message. This appeal expands the scope of rhetoric beyond the mere knowledge of the subject matter to encompass the credibility, character, and authority of the speaker. The third and final appeal in rhetoric, Pathos, uses loaded language to evoke emotions in the audience. It is commonly described as emotional persuasion, as it relies on the audience's emotional response to the message. In Aristotle's words, people are "led to feel emotion [*Pathos*] by the speech; for we do not give the same judgment when grieved and rejoicing or when being friendly and hostile", as cited in Jamar (2001: 71).

The three modes of persuasion highlight the ancient Greek scholars' profound recognition of the power of language and its capacity to effectively convey these distinct modes. Within each mode, a specific aspect of language is utilized, enabling the speaker to seamlessly transition from employing rational language for reasoning to forging empathetic connections with the audience through emotional language and ultimately establishing credibility through self-reference.

Returning to the history of political communication, Cicero (106–43 BC), the renowned Roman political leader, orator, lawyer, and philosopher, believed that perfect orators must combine eloquence and wisdom to effectively communicate their ideas (Ballacci 2018: 184). In his view, a perfect orator should possess "the subtlety of a logician, the thoughts of the philosopher, a diction almost poetic, a lawyer's memory, a tragedian's voice, and the bearing of the most consummate actor" (Cicero 1976b: xxviii, quoted by Gronbeck 2004: 139). In all these skills, language assumes a central role, operating at various levels encompassing cognition, memory, conceptual content, and effective delivery.

Machiavelli, the Italian Renaissance political thinker and statesman, was very critical of utopian philosophical schemes, such as those of Plato. His alternative perspectives laid the foundation for what would eventually be recognized as political pragmatism. Machiavelli's treatise is built on rejecting the moralistic view of authority and embracing the usage of all means at one's disposal, including rhetorical devices, to achieve one purpose, "control of public perceptions: public opinions, collective beliefs, shared feelings and emotional views of rulers themselves" (Gronbeck 2004: 140). In contemporary English, the term "Machiavellian" is frequently employed to describe any politician who is "indifferent to questions of morality, devotes himself to the pursuit of power" (Scruton 2007: 411).

During the 19th century, representative governments emerged, and citizens began to organize themselves into political parties and lobbying groups. Along with formal institutions, public spheres emerged during this period, where ongoing dialogues on public issues helped shape public opinion. The 20th century saw a significant intensification of language in politics, primarily thanks to two factors: first, the advent of radio and television as new means of political communication, and second, an increase in the number of voters. Politicians capitalized on these developments to reach a broader audience, making political communication faster, more frequent, and more mediatized. Nevertheless, communication involves a reciprocal exchange of information, attitudes, and opinions between rulers and their citizens. However, from the citizens' standpoint, communication often fell short of the ideal of a negotiated or deliberative style of governance. Orwell's concept of Newspeak captures this atmosphere, wherein the potential of language is reduced, making it difficult for citizens to express dissent or communicate ideas that deviate from the official narratives.

In addition, the atrocities of the two World Wars and the Cold War prompted political scientists and language researchers to examine the manipulative impact of political language, highlighting the need for greater awareness of how words were used to understate some facts and overstate others. These scholars asserted that governments disseminated false information to alleviate and even hide war atrocities. In his seminal work on public opinion, Lippmann (1997: 163) created a parallel between words and money, asserting that communication between conflicting nations was plagued by "a war fluctuation on word exchanges". Along the same lines, Orwell (1968) observed that political messages became vague, deceptive, and misleading because of the excessive use of metaphors, similes, and idioms. In the same way, McGinniss (1969) argued that the line between voting and selling had become blurred. In his book, *The Selling of a President*, he raised concerns about how political actors and campaigns adopt techniques originally designed for marketing in shaping public perceptions, engaging with voters, and promoting their agendas. This concern stems from the potential risks associated with applying marketing language to politics, as it may result in a shift in the perception of a president from a virtuous ruler with political aspirations to that of a commercial product with consumer attributes. Under the influence of marketing language, political language has been framed in dubious terms, such as "'strategic communication', 'political marketing', 'advertising', 'public diplomacy', and 'psychological operations'" (Robinson 2019: 10). The impact of marketing language has been maximized by the modern mass-media culture. Political discourse has become more conversational and professional (Fetzer & Bull 2012: 4). The mass-media culture has imposed its language style on politicians, leading political discourse, which was once centered around truth and virtue, to become entrenched in "a culture that requires *inflated* rhetoric" (Billig & MacMillan 2005: 478).

References to political actors, thus far, have been overly general, encompassing a wide range of individuals involved in political activities. The following section narrows the scope to American presidents and their specific discursive practices, as observed in their inaugural addresses.

4.3 The inaugural addresses and their generic properties

American presidents deliver six key speeches to communicate with the public, including an acceptance speech, an inaugural address, and four State of the Union speeches. Though these speeches receive nearly equal attention from scholars, the scope of this study is limited to inaugurals. These addresses are delivered by the president-elect on the inauguration day and serve as the first communication to the public at the start of a new presidential term.

The study of the American inaugurals falls within the presidential rhetoric scholarship. This field started in the 1980s, thanks to Ceaser et al. (1981) and Tulis (1987). Following these pioneering works, more research was conducted by scholars such as Hart (1987) and Campbell and Jamieson (1985). Around the early 1990s, case studies began to emerge, thanks to the works of Medhurst (1996), Stuckey and Antczak (1998), Medhurst and Aune (2008), and Dorsey (2008).

This field, the presidential rhetoric scholarship, refers to the academic study of the presidents' persuasive techniques, rhetorical devices, framing strategies, and linguistic choices and their impact on public opinion. Scholars in this field may emphasize certain aspects while downplaying others, but they all agree that presidents are expected to demonstrate exceptional persuasive skills. In fact, the concept of the "president as a persuader", coined by Windt (1986: 102), has gained widespread acceptance. This concept highlights the crucial role of language in the exercise of power, with a president's words often carrying greater weight than their deeds.

The interest of researchers in the president's words started when American presidents changed their communication styles. Presidents used to communicate with Congress in the constitutional presidency phase, whereas, in the rhetorical presidency phase, they began to appeal directly to the people. More specifically, this shift describes President Wilson and President Roosevelt's new communication style, which diverged from a traditional model of presidential leadership into a public-speaking model (Broughton 2009; Saldin 2011; Teten 2003). These two presidents went "over the heads" of Congress in order to promote themselves directly to the people (Stuckey 2010: 40).

Even if American presidents have become accustomed to direct communication with their people, the inaugural addresses nurtured long-established traditions and developed distinctive generic properties. Typically, an inaugural address has to convey a sense of stability and unity while simultaneously inspiring the public with a vision of progress and innovation. As Hinckley (1990: 24) notes, "[T]he inaugural must ensure continuity, but must also promise change". This particular generic property was first observed by Campbell and Jamieson (1985: 406), who contended that "the great inaugurals dramatically illustrate the processes of change within a continuous tradition".

The continuity trends are inherent in the epideictic nature of the inaugural ceremony. Epideictic discourse, in general, is audience-centered in which the speaker seeks to establish a connection with the audience by evoking shared emotions and creating a sense of identification or commonality. Moreover, these speeches have been consistently delivered within the same communication context since their inception, as Schaffner (1997: 3) notes. Theoretically, they occur within the same ceremonial setting (the inauguration ceremony), delivered by the same public figure (the president), directed towards the same recipients (the American people), and aimed, to a large extent, at achieving the same purpose(s). This continuity of form and structure often generates a sense of stability, as illustrated by the reiteration of familiar themes and values.

The trends of change, however, are not solely determined by prevailing circumstances; they are also influenced by the tradition that each elected president must articulate their policies, often aiming to bridge divisions and foster a collective sense of purpose through the rhetoric of hope and unity. In other words, these speeches represent a complex blend of "relatively stable cognitive frames" and new ones (Martin 2015: 27).

In addition to maintaining the balance between continuity and change, American presidents, like other politicians in pluralist democracies, must balance their "passion for distinction", to borrow President Adams' words, with "the necessity of agreement and compromise" (Ballacci 2018: 171). This tension between individual ambition and collective responsibility is mirrored in the linguistic choices made by presidents, wherein the power of language is evident in both showcasing stylistic excellence and distinction, and effectively conveying a clear, plain, and coherent message to the public. Being an orator is undoubtedly an esteemed quality, but being a wise politician entails recognizing when "to avoid fine oratory in favor of a rhetorical style that sounds un-rhetorical, seeming to be plain factually-informative speech" (Kane & Patapan 2010: 371).

In terms of content, the inaugural addresses share some distinctive thematic features. In each inaugural address, the new elect U.S. president is expected to express commitment to upholding American ideals, defending the Constitution, safeguarding the union, and promoting federalism domestically while leading by example on the global stage. Central to this mission is the recognition that its realization hinges upon two critical factors. The first pertains to the cultivation of a virtuous, nonpartisan, and cohesive citizenry, while the second involves the active cooperation of Congress, the divine providence of God, and the support of the people at large.

Identifying genre-specific features contributes to our understanding of how presidents establish effective communication with their citizens. While efficient communication may appear straightforward, politicians and linguists, among others, are aware of the sensitivity of words. Chilton and Schaffner (2011: 304) assert that "the meaning of words has traditionally raised problems and caused anxieties". Rhetorical effectiveness, however, requires the use of words to solve problems and alleviate anxieties. To this end, politicians often employ metaphors, as framing and reasoning devices, to make their conceptualizations more appealing and accessible to a wider public. Given the book's focus on metaphor-related prepositions, the forthcoming section examines how metaphorical framing operates in political discourse and, more specifically, in American inaugural addresses.

4.4 Conceptual metaphors in political discourse

Political metaphors are not just figures of speech extracted from political texts but metaphors that are "used with a political goal, that is creating political expectations and/or realizing political objectives and actions" (Reuchamps, Thibodeau & Perrez 2019: 5). These metaphors shape how we perceive and interpret political issues and events and influence our decisions in response to them. For instance, politicians use metaphors to define their country's enemies and determine the appropriate course of action to deal with them.

In his attempt to classify political metaphors, Chilton (2006) argues that they are mainly structured by these five image schemata: FRONT-BACK, UP-DOWN, PATH, CONTAINER, and CENTER-PERIPHERY. The first image schema accounts for metaphors that organize people and ideas in terms of importance and priority. The UP-DOWN image schema structures most of the concepts of hierarchy. Through these metaphors, we link power, prestige, and vitality with being UP, while we associate weakness, shame, and decay with being DOWN. The PATH image schema is usually related to the metaphors of progress, where politicians conceptualize their efforts to attain specific objectives as forward motion along a path leading to specific destinations. As for the fourth image schema, the CONTAINER schema imposes its boundaries (inside/outside) on situations involving political concepts, actors, and institutions. For example, it is commonly used to conceptualize a country as a container-like entity with locals as insiders and immigrants as outsiders. Through this metaphor, politicians create a sense of belonging and identity for those within the container and a sense of exclusion and othering for those outside it. Finally, the CENTER-PERIPHERY image schema is used to conceptualize power and authority at the heart of a network, radiating influence outward to the periphery. Those at the center enjoy greater status and prestige, while those on the periphery are less important or less influential, relegated to the margins of society.

In addition to image schemas, specific source domains have been identified as frequently employed in political discourse. They include family, journey, life-health-body, and architecture-house-building (Musolff 2004a: 69), as well as the human body, ships, machines, and buildings (Chilton 2006: 65), and war, business, family, person, and race (Kövecses 2010: 68).

More specifically, Charteris-Black (2004) studied the inaugurals' metaphors and identified seven source domains: conflict, journey, building, light and fire, physical environment, religion, and body. The conflict domain motivates military or war metaphors to conceptualize political action in terms of a military operation in which politicians fight for good social goals and against social ills. As for journeys, they are often projected onto objectives to be attained. The domain of buildings emphasizes the establishment of well-founded principles such as peace, democracy, and progress. Traditionally, light and fire have been associated with understanding and emotion, respectively. While light is necessary for seeing and thus understanding, darkness is mapped onto "ignorance, failure to understand and evil" (Charteris-Black 2004: 101). The contrast between light and darkness motivates metaphors that deal with "moral notions of goodness and evil" (Charteris-Black 2004: 102). Metaphors of the physical environment can be categorized into two domains: weather and geography. The former is used to convey metaphors of change, either positive or negative. The latter domain of the physical environment, geography, is related to metaphors dealing with the social situations of people, countries, or individuals. The vertical or horizontal features of natural phenomena are highlighted to convey concepts of effort and distance, respectively. Religion is the sixth source domain in Charteris-Black's list. It is mapped onto politics in a way that "links the president with a commitment to Christian religious belief" (Charteris-Black 2004: 103–104). The seventh and final source domain encompasses body parts that give rise to metaphors and metonymies related to body politics. In this framework, the State and its institutions are metaphorically conceptualized as a biological body, wherein different body parts correspond to different political actors.

Looking at the figures that support Charteris-Black's results, conflict metaphors represent 36% of all metaphors in inaugurals. This significant percentage sets a confrontational and aggressive tone for the inaugurals. However, this tone may not be appropriate for the nature of the discourse situation. Inaugurals are delivered after the elections and are meant to unify the nation rather than provoke conflict and division. Furthermore, Charteris-Black's results do not make any references to metaphor variation influenced by historical factors. As a historical text, these addresses typically reflect a diachronic evolution of their main concepts. Therefore, the next section outlines the major trends in the evolution of presidential communication within the framework of diachronic studies of metaphor variation.

4.5 The evolution trends of inaugural addresses

Throughout history, there have been significant changes in the way American presidents communicate with the public. In the 19th century, the prevailing norm was "presidential humility" (Ericson 1997), which aligned with the image of a president who adhered strictly to the Constitution. However, the emergence of the rhetorical presidency under President Wilson marked a turning point in American political culture. Rather than relying solely on the support of Congress, American presidents began to cultivate a closer relationship with the public through their speeches.

The rise of the rhetorical presidency has brought about significant changes in presidential communication style. Lim (2002: 346) identified five trends in modern American presidential rhetoric. According to these trends, American presidents have become (1) anti-intellectual; (2) more abstract; (3) more assertive; (4) more democratic, and (5) more conversational.

As for the first trend, late 20th-century American presidents show "reverence of the opinion, judgment, and rhetoric of the common man" (Lim 2002: 333). Moreover, in terms of linguistic choices, these presidents started to use colloquial words more than formal ones. To demonstrate the shift towards an anti-intellectual style, Lim (2002: 334) compared two conceptualizations of liberty. For President Harrison, liberty is "the sovereign balm for every injury which our institutions may receive", while for President Bush, it is "like a beautiful kite that can go higher and higher with the breeze". In conjunction with its anti-intellectual trend, modern American presidential rhetoric grew more abstract. Three main types of abstract concepts have been widely used, namely "religious, poetic and idealistic". The presence of these "lofty" concepts in anti-intellectual rhetoric is considered "awkward" by Lim (2002). The overall effect is rhetoric with vacuous ideas that require "pontification without explanation" (Lim 2002: 334). Indeed, this type of rhetoric that relies heavily on such high principles and concepts is often called the "rhetoric of assent" (Booth 1974). Consider, for example, President Bush's words: "America has never been united by blood or birth or soil. We are bound by ideals that move us beyond our backgrounds, lift us above our interests and teach us what it means to be citizens" (Bush 2001). The use of overly grandiose language and vague, empty phrases creates an impression that the President's words are "utterly unassailable" (Lim 2002: 335). As for the assertive tone of the modern American presidential rhetoric, Lim (2002: 337) observed that it has become "activist, realist and confident". The rhetorical assertiveness is exemplified through words related to "active orientation", "strength", "power", "influence", "commencement", "renewal", "reform", and "hope". At the same time, Lim (2002: 337) observed a steady decline in references to "passivity", "submission", "uncertainty", "vagueness", "providence", and "fate". Regarding the fourth trend, the rhetoric of modern American presidents promotes "people-oriented" and democratic ideals according to which presidents are portrayed as "protectors and defenders of the people" (Lim 2002: 339). Thus, modern American presidents have become more concerned about the less fortunate sections of society. They started to refer more to the people, previous presidents, themselves, and less to other government branches and even the Constitution. As for the tendency to express democratic ideals, the relationship between American presidents and the public has changed from "authority to comradeship" (Lim 2002: 341). Consequently, democratic rhetoric evolved into a tool to "convey and persuade, not command and overawe", as Kane and Patapan (2010: 371) put it. The fifth and final trend in modern American presidential rhetoric is a shift towards a more "conversational" communication style (Lim 2002: 346). In this style, presidents aim to establish their trustworthiness with the audience through the use of personal anecdotes and self-references.

In the present day, the digital age has further transformed the image of the presidency, as well as the role and tactics of American presidents in persuasion. With social media and other digital tools, presidents have unprecedented access to the public and can communicate with their citizens in real time. This has led to new challenges and opportunities for presidents to shape public opinion and influence policy outcomes.

While these trends illustrate the evolving nature of presidential rhetoric, it is important to note that the use of conceptual metaphors has experienced a similar evolution. The following section will explore the literature on diachronic linguistics and how conceptual mappings have evolved over time.

4.6 Metaphor variation and diachronic approach

The study of metaphor variation has been referred to by various labels such as "history of ideas" or "directional paths of semantic change" (Sweetser 1987: 446), "conceptual history" of metaphors (Musolff 2004b: 55), and "historical approach on metaphor" (Zhang, Geeraerts & Speelman 2015: 291). Despite the differences in terminology, these labels reflect the same underlying interest in exploring how metaphors evolve over time. The terms "historical" and "diachronic" are often used interchangeably in the literature on metaphor variation, while the term "evolutionary" is gaining popularity as it describes the gradual and incremental changes that occur in the meanings of words and phrases over time. The variety of terms highlights the fact that this field is "still relatively unexplored" (Trim 2011: xi), and it "has not or not yet shown any visible theoretic or practical progress" (Rastier 1999: 110). In Sweetser's words, "meaning-change remains perhaps the least understood area of linguistic change" (Sweetser 1987: 447).

In general, metaphor variation studies rest on the idea that present-day linguistic expressions are the outcome of a series of gradual historical evolution. As (Bybee 2007) argues, "all synchronic states are the result of a long chain of diachronic developments". For instance, Kövecses (2006: 1–5) has traced the evolution of the ANGER IS HEAT metaphor from Old English to Middle English, demonstrating significant changes in its usage and meanings. Similarly, the MIND AS BODY metaphor has undergone a significant transformation over the centuries, evolving from the Chariot Allegory in ancient times to the computer as a source domain in contemporary discourse.

These diachronic developments, however, seem to be at odds with the stability of universal metaphors. In other words, the main question is whether universal conceptual metaphors are diachronically constant. The answer is not straightforward as long as the dichotomy between the basis of metaphor and the context of metaphor is unresolved. On the one hand, the embodiment principle renders metaphors invariable. Basic cognitive domains such as space and time are "cognitively irreducible, neither derivable from nor analyzable into other conceptions" (Langacker 2008: 44), and they, therefore, tend to stabilize metaphors and obstruct their variations. On the other hand, the embodiment principle also includes social and historical fluctuations that render metaphors susceptible to variations. The present study is aware of these conflicting tendencies, and it, therefore, assumes that metaphor-related prepositions can manifest a compromise between these tendencies, thanks to the prepositions' constant image-schematic structure, as well as the variable semantic fields evoked by the trajectors and landmarks.

In order to explain how metaphors vary, Kövecses (2006: 3) coined the term "differential experiential focus". Accordingly, variations occur when different components receive various degrees of focus in different historical periods. Trim (2007: xiii) expanded this concept to include "the nature of saliency at a given point in time" and, more precisely, the concept of diachronic salience. Diachronic salience refers to the relative prominence of specific conceptual mappings over a given period. When a particular conceptual mapping is considered salient, it means that it was once commonly and frequently used. However, the salience of a particular conceptual mapping can undergo changes, including a loss of prominence leading to obsolescence, a temporary decline followed by a resurgence, or fluctuations in its level of prominence. The study of diachronic salience aims to trace the changes and evolution of conceptual mappings across historical stages while also investigating the factors that contribute to these transformations. More specifically, the salience of one conceptual mapping over another "depends on a variety of factors in the surrounding cultural context" (Kövecses 2006: 5). These factors make metaphors open to "culturally-based interpretations" (Trim 2011: 11).

This book assumes that "many of our basic conceptual metaphors, together with their various linguistic derivations, do have specific models of evolution" (Trim 2007: xiii). This assumption is, in its turn, built on Trim's extensive investigation into the evolution of conceptual mappings throughout European history. In order to explore the different aspects of conceptual diachronic evolution, Trim (2011: 24) developed an "Evolutionary Model of Conceptual Mapping" with six parameters, as illustrated in Figure 4.1.

According to Trim's model, any conceptual mapping has an evolutionary path influenced by six interconnected parameters. First, basic conceptualization processes, including sensory perception and embodiment, can have a direct impact on diachronic trends. Second, language structures play a role in shaping our thoughts and the metaphors we generate. The third parameter, which pertains to universal mechanisms, indicates that conceptual mappings based on physiological features typically exhibit long-term paths. Fourth, levels of diachronic salience may rise and fall over time. As for the fifth parameter, the semantic fields invoked to structure certain metaphors can fluctuate in terms of salience. The sixth and final parameter is about cultural variants which interact with other parameters and influence the evolution of conceptual mappings.

In addition to these parameters, Trim's model can be enriched by incorporating a seventh parameter that considers genre constraints. In the context of inaugural addresses, the new parameter would encompass their generic properties related to their purpose, structure, style, language, and rhetorical devices. These properties serve as variables that influence both long- and short-term diachronic paths. By taking these factors into account,

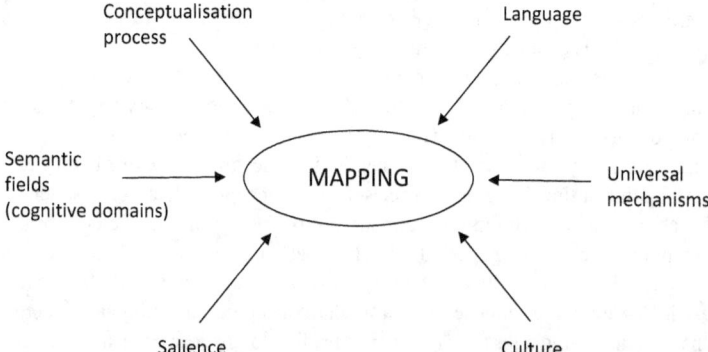

Figure 4.1 The six-parameter evolutionary model of conceptual mapping by Trim (2011: 24).

we can delve into the diachronic trends of metaphor-related prepositions, examining when their usage increased or declined and identifying the factors that contributed to their evolution.

References

Ballacci, Giuseppe. 2018. *Political theory between philosophy and rhetoric. Politics as transcendence and contingency*. London, England: Palgrave Macmillan.

Bayley, Paul. 2005. Analysing language and politics. *Mediazioni: Online Journal of Interdisciplinary Studies of Language and Cultures* 1–9. https://mediazioni.sitlec. unibo.it/images/stories/PDF_folder/document-pdf/2005/articoli2005/4%20bayley.pdf

Billig, Michael & Katie MacMillan. 2005. Metaphor, idiom and ideology: The search for "no smoking guns" across time. *Discourse & Society* 16(4). 459–480.

Booth, Wayne C. 1974. *Modern dogma and the rhetoric of assent*. Chicago, IL: The University of Chicago Press.

Broughton, J. Richard. 2009. The inaugural address as constitutional statesmanship. *Quinnipiac Law Review* 28. 265–320.

Bush, George W. 2001. First Inaugural Address. *The American Presidency Project*. https://www.presidency.ucsb.edu/documents/inaugural-address-52 (24 January, 2017).

Bybee, Joan L. 2007. Diachronic linguistics. In Geeraerts, Dirk & Cuyckens, Hubert (ed.), *The Oxford handbook of cognitive linguistics*, 945–987. New York, NY: Oxford University Press.

Campbell, Karlyn Kohrs & Kathleen Hall Jamieson. 1985. Inaugurating the presidency. *Presidential Studies Quarterly* 15(2). 394–411.

Ceaser, James W., Glenn E. Thurow, Jeffrey Tulis & Joseph M. Bessette. 1981. The rise of the rhetorical presidency. *Presidential Studies Quarterly* 11(2). 158–171.

Charteris-Black, Jonathan. 2004. *Corpus approaches to critical metaphor analysis*. 1st edn. New York, NY: Palgrave MacMillan.

Chilton, Paul. 2006. Metaphors in political discourse. In Brown, Keith (ed.), *Encyclopedia of language and linguistics*, 63–65. 2nd edn. Oxford, England: The UK, Elsevier Science & Technology.

Chilton, Paul & Christina Schaffner. 2011. Discourse and politics. In Van Dijk, Teun A. (ed.), *Discourse studies: A multidisciplinary introduction*, 303–330. London, England: Sage.

Connolly, William E. 1993. *The terms of political discourse*. 3rd edn. New Jersey, NJ: Princeton University Press.

Dorsey, Leroy G. 2008. *The presidency and rhetorical leadership*. (Ed.) Dorsey, Leroy G. College Station: Texas A&M University Press.

Ericson, David F. 1997. Presidential inaugural addresses and American political culture. *Presidential Studies Quarterly*. Center for the Study of the Presidency 27(4). 727–744.

Fairclough, Norman & Isabela Fairclough. 2012. *Political discourse analysis: A method for advanced students*. 1st edn. London, England: Routledge.

Fetzer, Anita & Peter Bull. 2012. Doing leadership in political speech: Semantic processes and pragmatic inferences. *Discourse & Society* 23(2). 127–144.

Gronbeck, Bruce E. 2004. Rhetoric and politics. In Kaid, Lynda Lee (ed.), *Handbook of political communication research*, 135–154. New Jersey, NJ: Lawrence Erlbaum Associates.

Hart, Roderick P. 1987. *The sound of leadership: Presidential communication in the modern age*. Chicago, IL: University of Chicago Press.
Herman, Edward S. & Noam Chomsky. 1988. *Manufacturing consent: The political economy of the mass media*. New York, NY: Pantheon Books.
Hinckley, Barbara. 1990. *The symbolic presidency: How presidents portray themselves*. New York, NY: Routledge.
Hornikx, Jos Mathieu Albert. 2005. *Cultural differences in the persuasiveness of evidence types in France and the Netherlands*. [Doctoral dissertation, Radboud University].
Jamar, Steven D. 2001. Aristotle teaches persuasion: The psychic connection. *Journal of Legal Writing* 8. 61–102.
Jucker, Andreas H. 1997. Persuasion by inference: Analysis of a party political broadcast. In Blommaert, Jan & Bulcaen, Chris (ed.), *Political linguistics*, 121–137. Amsterdam, The Netherlands: John Benjamins.
Kane, John & Haig Patapan. 2010. The artless art: Leadership and the limits of democratic rhetoric. *Australian Journal of Political Science* 45(3). 371–389.
Kövecses, Zoltán. 2006. Embodiment, experiential focus, and diachronic change in metaphor. In McConchie, Roderick, Timofeeva, Olga, Tissari, Heli & Säily, Tanja (ed.), *Selected Proceedings of the 2005 Symposium on New Approaches in English Historical Lexis (HEL-LEX)*, 1–7. Somerville, MA: Cascadilla Proceedings Project.
Kövecses, Zoltán. 2010. *Metaphor: A practical introduction*. 2nd edn. Oxford, England: Oxford University Press.
Langacker, Ronald W. 2008. *Cognitive grammar: A basic introduction*. Oxford, England: Oxford University Press.
Lim, Elvin T. 2002. Five trends in presidential rhetoric: An analysis of rhetoric from George Washington to Bill Clinton. *Presidential Studies Quarterly*. Wiley Online Library 32(2). 328–348.
Lippmann, Walter. 1997. *Public opinion*. New York, NY: The Free Press.
Martin, James. 2015. Situating speech: A rhetorical approach to political strategy. *Political Studies*. SAGE Publications Sage UK: London, England 63(1). 25–42.
McGinniss, Joe. 1969. *The selling of the president*. New York, NY: Trident Press.
Medhurst, Martin J. 1996. *Beyond the rhetorical presidency*. (Ed.) Medhurst, Martin J. College Station: Texas A&M University Press.
Medhurst, Martin J. & James Arnt Aune. 2008. *The prospect of presidential rhetoric*. (Ed.) Medhurst, Martin J. and Aune, James Arnt. College Station: Texas A&M University Press.
Musolff, Andreas. 2004a. *Metaphor and political discourse: Analogical reasoning in debates about Europe*. New York, NY: Palgrave Macmillan.
Musolff, Andreas. 2004b. Metaphor and conceptual evolution. *Metaphorik.de* 7. 55–75.
Orwell, George. 1968. Politics and the English language. In Orwell, Sonia & Angos, Ian (ed.), *The collected essays, journalism and letters of George Orwell*, 127–140. New York, NY: Harcourt.
Rastier, François. 1999. Cognitive semantics and diachronic semantics: The values and evolution of classes. In Blank, Andreas & Koch, Peter (ed.), *Historical semantics and cognition*, 109–144. Berlin, Germany: De Gruyter.
Reuchamps, Min, Paul H. Thibodeau & Julien Perrez. 2019. Studying variation in political metaphor: From discourse analysis to experiment. In Reuchamps, Min,

Thibodeau, Paul H. & Perrez, Julien (ed.), *Variation in political metaphor*, 1–11. Amsterdam, The Netherlands: John Benjamins Publishing Company.

Ringmar, Erik. 2007. The power of metaphor: Consent, dissent and revolution. In Mole, Richard C. M. (ed.), *Discursive constructions of identity in European politics*, 119–136. 1st edn. London, England: Palgrave Macmillan.

Robinson, Piers Gregory. 2019. Expanding the field of political communication: Making the case for critical propaganda studies. *Frontiers in Communication*. Frontiers 4(26). 1–13.

Saldin, Robert P. 2011. William McKinley and the rhetorical presidency. *Presidential Studies Quarterly* 41(1). 119–134.

Schaffner, Christina. 1997. *Analysing political speeches*. Clevedon, England: Multilingual Matters.

Scruton, Roger. 2007. *Dictionary of political thought*. 3rd edn. New York, NY: Palgrave Macmillan.

Stuckey, Mary E. 2010. Rethinking the rhetorical presidency and presidential rhetoric. *Review of Communication* 10(1). 38–52.

Stuckey, Mary E. & Frederick J. Antczak. 1998. The rhetorical presidency: Deepening vision, widening exchange. In Roloff, M. (ed.), *Communication yearbook 21*, 405–442. New York, NY: Routledge.

Sweetser, Eve E. 1987. Metaphorical models of thought and speech: a comparison of historical directions and metaphorical mappings in the two domains. In *Proceedings of the Thirteenth Annual Meeting of the Berkeley Linguistics Society*, 446–459. Berkeley, CA: eLanguage. http://linguistics.berkeley.edu/bls/.

Teten, Ryan L. 2003. Evolution of the modern rhetorical presidency: Presidential presentation and development of the State of the Union address. *Presidential Studies Quarterly*. Wiley Online Library 33(2). 333–346.

Trim, Richard. 2007. *Metaphor networks: The comparative evolution of figurative language*. Basingstoke, England: Palgrave Macmillan.

Trim, Richard. 2011. *Metaphor and the historical evolution of conceptual mapping*. Basingstoke, England: Palgrave Macmillan.

Tulis, Jeffrey. 1987. *The rhetorical presidency*. Princeton, NJ: Princeton University Press.

Windt, Theodore Otto. 1986. Presidential rhetoric: Definition of a field of study. *Presidential Studies Quarterly* 16(1). 102–116.

Zhang, Weiwei, Dirk Geeraerts & Dirk Speelman. 2015. Visualizing onomasiological change: Diachronic variation in metonymic patterns for WOMAN in Chinese. *Cognitive Linguistics*. De Gruyter 26(2). 289–330.

5 A prepositional portrait
Corpus and frequency

5.1 Corpus linguistics and metaphor research

By adopting a quantitative methodology, cognitive linguistics has undergone a significant transformation (Geeraerts 2010). The corpus-based approach has been influential in demonstrating the multifaceted nature of metaphor and in advancing our understanding of its various dimensions (Semino 2017). This approach offers "explicit procedures, and not just intuitive judgments" (Gibbs 2011). These procedures have proven useful for extracting linguistic metaphors from large corpora, quantifying their frequency, and proving the major claims about metaphor, such as its ubiquity, systematicity of mappings, and conceptual domains (Wikberg 2008).

Corpus-based approaches in metaphor studies warrant greater attention due to their popularity and usefulness. Unfortunately, this brief outline does not do justice to their significance due to space limitations. However, having emphasized the importance of these approaches, the remaining sections will concentrate on the Inaugural Corpus.

5.2 The Inaugural Corpus

The term "Inaugural Corpus" is used in this book to refer to the complete collection of inaugural speeches of American presidents from 1789 to 2021. These speeches are delivered by elected presidents following a public ceremony during which they take the oath of office. In the literature, this same Corpus is often assigned various labels, such as the "US Inaugural Corpus" by Charteris-Black (2004: 88), the "U.S. Presidential Inaugural Address Corpus" by Lewis and Grossetti (2022), and the "Inaugural Address Corpus" by Bird, Klein, and Loper (2009).

The Inaugural Corpus has the following five characteristics: first, it is a monolingual corpus since all inaugurals were originally written and delivered in English. Second, it is an original corpus with no translations or adaptations of the speeches included. Third, this Corpus is of a diachronic nature as it spans over 232 years. Thus, it falls into the category of "historical corpus data"

DOI: 10.4324/9781003369646-5

(Zhang, Geeraerts & Speelman 2015: 291). Fourth, this Corpus is dynamic, constantly expanding at a "predictable frequency" (Rowley 2010: 44). Following the election of a new president every four years, a new speech is delivered during the inaugural ceremony. Consequently, a new text is added to the Inaugural Corpus every four years. Finally, this Corpus is unique as it consists exclusively of a specific genre written by specific authors. In contrast, a general corpus encompasses various texts from different genres and serves as a representation of a particular language. The Inaugural Corpus does not fully represent the entirety of the English language. However, it does capture the specific language employed by American presidents in their inaugural addresses.

As for data collection procedures, the 59 inaugural addresses were collected from the American Presidency Project, a website managed by the University of California, Santa Barbara. (http://www.presidency.ucsb.edu/inaugurals.php). To ensure accuracy, all the extracted addresses were cross-checked against another reliable source, the Avalon Project (http://avalon.law.yale.edu/subject menus/inaug.asp). The Inaugural Corpus, consisting of 59 texts, comprises a total of 138,454 words. The average length of these inaugural addresses is 2,347 words, and the median word count, which represents the middle value of the distribution, is 2,120 words. However, the average and the median may not be representative of the typical speech length as the range of word counts is quite extensive. The wide range illustrates a substantial variability in speech lengths within the Corpus. The shortest address comprises only 135 words, whereas the longest extends to 8,460 words. When analyzing the distribution of speeches based on their word count, 30 speeches have a word count ranging between 1,335 and 2,535 words. The remaining speeches are distributed as follows: 11 speeches have word counts below 1,335 words, indicating relatively shorter addresses, and 18 speeches exceed 2,535 words, indicating longer speeches. In terms of their historical distribution, 3 addresses were delivered during the 18th century, 25 addresses were delivered in both the 19th and 20th centuries, and so far, 6 addresses have been delivered in the 21st century.

The extracted addresses have been converted into text files to ensure compatibility with the analytical tools' requirements. Any extraneous information, such as symbols, images, and HTML codes, has been removed. After being cleaned, the files contain only the transcripts of the original addresses. These files were labeled according to their respective delivery dates and then saved into 59.*txt* files. In this way, the Inaugural Corpus has been saved in a digital format, making it machine-readable. It can be accessed either as a folder containing the whole Corpus or as separate files containing the individual transcripts of the inaugurals. Then, they were loaded into *AntConc* for quantitative analysis. The software *AntConc* is a concordance program that grants researchers access to texts within a corpus, facilitating the analysis of language phenomena through various functions, including concordance, clustering, N-Gram, collocation, and keyword lists (Anthony 2022).

The next step is to conduct search queries in *AntConc* by entering a search word in the designated search box. The search words, in this case, are English one-word prepositions. Each preposition was searched individually, and with each search, the software computed the total hits indicating the number of occurrences of that specific preposition in the Inaugural Corpus. Furthermore, the software displayed the preposition in its context using the Key Word in Context (KWIC) function, and it also showed the occurrences of each preposition in every speech using the File View function. The keywords consisted of precisely 74 one-word prepositions, extracted from two primary sources: (Carter & McCarthy 2006: 251) and (Leech, Rayson & others 2001: 294).

The following section will present the results of the queries and analyze the distribution of these 74 prepositions in the Inaugural Corpus.

5.3   The prepositions' frequency patterns

The Inaugural Corpus features 66 out of the 74 prepositions. This means that eight prepositions have not been observed in this Corpus. These 66 prepositions account for a total of 22,840 tokens, representing 16.5% of the entire Corpus.

The values of each preposition exhibit a significant dispersion, with scores ranging widely from 7,189 to 1. Furthermore, the standard deviation is remarkably high, reaching 1,044. This obvious disparity indicates that the

Table 5.1 Distribution of the 66 repositions by frequency range

Group	Members	Frequency Range (Actual Range)
A	of	Above 5,000 (7,189)
B	to, in	2,001–5,000 (2,834–4,608)
C	for, by	1,001–2,000 (1,095–1,232)
D	as, with, from, on, upon, at	201–1,000 (375–971)
E	under, without, before, into, through, against, among, out	101–200 (102–199)
F	between, within, over, like, up, since, toward, beyond, about, until, after, throughout, across, during, down, around, above, except, off, along	11–100 (15–98)
G	behind, near, concerning, amid, including, worth, amidst, save, amongst, despite, outside, till, beneath, regarding, unto, below, following, inside, notwithstanding, onto, touching, towards, versus, alongside, considering underneath, unlike	10 and below (1–10)

range is greatly influenced by these extreme outliers. Consequently, it is more informative to categorize these 66 prepositions into seven groups based on their observed frequencies. Table 5.1 illustrates these groups along with their respective prepositions and frequency ranges.

The 66 prepositions are grouped into different categories based on their frequency ranges to highlight their distribution patterns. One notable remark is the stark contrast in the frequency distribution of prepositions. Specifically, a small subset of prepositions exhibits remarkably high frequencies, while a vast majority of prepositions demonstrate considerably lower frequencies. This small subset consists of 11 prepositions whose frequencies are above 200 (groups A, B, C, and D). Conversely, there are 55 prepositions in groups E, F, and G that occurred less than 200 times in the Inaugural Corpus. When visually presented, the uneven distribution of prepositions takes a pyramid-like shape, as illustrated in Figure 5.1. The summit of this pyramid comprises a small number of highly frequent prepositions, while the base consists of a large number of less frequent ones.

In terms of percentage, the distribution of prepositions in the Inaugural Corpus is uneven. Specifically, only 16.7% of the prepositions account for 90.8% of the total number of occurrences, while 83.3% of the prepositions account for only 9.2%. Table 5.2 provides an additional visual representation of the unequal distribution by presenting the relative proportions of each group in the Inaugural Corpus.

The data presented in Table 5.2 reveal the following four key observations:

1 The dominant prepositions: a select few prepositions are widely utilized, accounting for more than 90% of the occurrences. These 11 dominant prepositions play a central role in the language employed within the Inaugural Corpus.

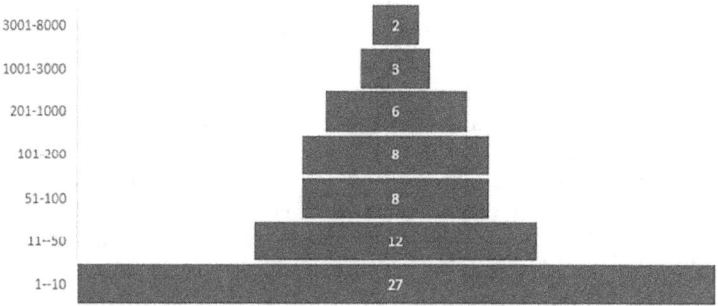

Figure 5.1 The frequency distribution of prepositions in the Inaugural Corpus.

Table 5.2 Distribution of preposition occurrences across the seven groups

Groups	Count of Prepositions	Occurrences	% of All Occurrences
A	1	7,189	31.5
B	2	7,442	32.6
C+D	8	6,125	26.8
E+F+G	55	2,098	9.2
Total	66	22,854	100

2 The marginal prepositions: a substantial number of prepositions are used with lower frequency, comprising a smaller proportion of the total occurrences. These 55 prepositions may be considered peripheral in the language used in the Inaugural Corpus.

3 The prevalent OF: this preposition stands out as the most frequent, outpacing other prepositions by a significant margin. Its prevalence implies that it plays a significant role in expressing relationships between entities and in other syntactic structures in the Inaugural Corpus.

4 The absent prepositions: eight prepositions were not observed at all in the Inaugural Corpus. They are as follows: OPPOSITE, ABOARD, BESIDE, MINUS, PER, PLUS, ROUND, and VIA. Their absence indicates that these prepositions have never been needed in the syntactic structures and the topics being discussed.

The first three observations align with the findings of three previous studies on three distinct corpora. The first study is based on the British National Corpus (Leech, Rayson & others 2001). The second study analyzed a one-million-word sample from the Lancaster-Oslo/Bergen Corpus (LOB) (Johansson & Hofland 1989). Finally, the third study used both the Brown corpus for American English and the LOB corpus for British English (Mindt & Weber 1989). These three studies collectively reinforce the same usage patterns of English prepositions. First, they agree that there is a group of approximately ten prepositions with a high frequency. Interestingly, these prepositions align with those identified in the Inaugural Corpus (IN, TO, FOR, WITH, ON, BY, AT, FROM, and AS). Second, these studies also report a remarkable presence of a substantial number of prepositions with low frequencies. Third, they also highlight the prevalence of the preposition OF. As for the fourth observation concerning the absent prepositions, these three studies neither confirm nor contradict it. This implies that these studies consider zero scores not meaningful or problematic for statistical purposes.

Similarly, the aforementioned four observations are supported by diachronic studies examining the usage patterns of prepositions. These same usage patterns are observed in two studies on the distribution of 50 English prepositions over four periods: Old English, Middle English, Early Modern English, and Modern English. The first study, conducted by Rissanen et al. (1993: 1–17), investigates the diachronic section of the Helsinki Corpus, covering the data from the first three periods, while the second study, conducted by Leech, Rayson, and others (2001), focuses on Modern English data. By comparing the Inaugural Corpus with these diachronic studies, two key observations can be made. First, the 11 highly frequent prepositions in the Inaugural Corpus are consistent with those observed in both Modern and Early Modern English, as well as in Middle English. For instance, the prepositions IN and TO have consistently held the second and third positions, respectively, while FOR has maintained its fourth position since 1150. The fifth to eleventh positions are occupied by prepositions including BY, WITH, AS, FROM, ON, and AT, with varying rankings. The only preposition that does not appear in the other corpora is UPON. The second and final observation pertains to the preposition OF. It has maintained its status as the most frequently used preposition in English from 1150 to the present day.

The frequency scores of prepositions in the Inaugural Corpus reveal not only an uneven distribution but also a shift in the preposition-to-word ratio over time. The forthcoming section will provide a more detailed explanation of this point.

5.4 Tracking the preposition-to-word ratio

As depicted in the following graph, there has been a noticeable decline in this ratio throughout the historical progression of inaugurals (Figure 5.2).

The trend of preposition usage has seen a marked shift, moving towards a lower frequency over time. In the first inaugural address, the usage of prepositions accounted for approximately 18.4%, but in the latest speech, it only made up 13.3%. This steady decrease can be quantified by converting the

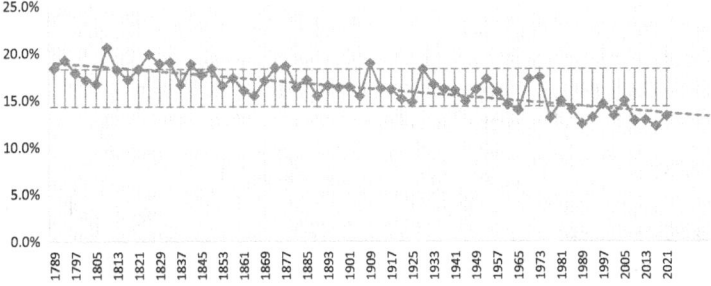

Figure 5.2 The ratio of all the prepositions over the history of the Inaugural Corpus.

percentages into ratio rates. The average ratio of prepositions to words was one preposition per every five words in the 18th and 19th centuries. However, in the 21st century, the ratio has dropped to one preposition per every eight words, indicating a significant decline in usage. For example, this decline can be clearly seen when comparing President Madison's 1809 address, which had a preposition-to-word ratio of 1 to 4, with President Biden's 2021 address, where the ratio was 1 to 8.

It is noteworthy that the length of the inaugural speeches has not decreased, making it inaccurate to conclude that the decrease in prepositions is due to shorter speeches. The decrease in the usage of prepositions is a distinct phenomenon that requires further examination. It is evident that a considerable number of sentences are now being constructed with fewer prepositions. A decrease in preposition usage corresponds to a decrease in noun usage. Hudson (1994: 336) observes that "every corpus which is high on prepositions and common nouns is low on verbs and pronouns, and vice versa". This correlation highlights a change in style, indicating a shift in the way language is being used and structured in American inaugurals. Prepositions serve as markers of style and tone, and a decrease in their usage signals a transition from a highly formal style to a less formal and even informal style. "Nouns, adjectives, articles, and prepositions are more frequent in formal styles", as Heylighen and Dewaele (1999: 1) observe in their empirical measure of formality.

Furthermore, there has been a trend towards using fewer nouns and prepositions in American inaugurals, indicating a shift towards a more conversational and informal mode of communication. These observations agree with the findings of Lim (2002: 333), who argues that modern American presidents tend "to substitute formal word choices for more colloquial turns of phrase". These stylistic changes mirror a tendency to develop a relatable and accessible approach to public speaking. This view is in line with Biber and Finegan (2001: 67), who argue that "English registers have been following a general 'drift' towards more oral styles over the last four centuries".

In addition to stylistic factors, inaugurals have undergone a transformation in their generic properties, evolving from written speeches intended for a small, intimate audience to a highly publicized media event broadcast to a global audience. American inaugurals started as oral texts to be heard. Then, thanks to the widespread use of printing, they developed into written texts to be read. Later, they became oral texts broadcasted via the radio, followed by televised events broadcasted on television. Finally, they evolved into digital content disseminated through the internet. Within the new digital-laden paradigm, public discourse has adjusted its choice of words to "the frame of the screen" (Samuels 2008: 232). When considering the epidictic aspect of American inaugurals, it appears that modern presidents tend to rely on ritualized, formulaic language that prioritizes shorter sentences. This means fewer nouns and, therefore, fewer prepositions, a style well suited to the media's requirements. It reflects the aesthetics of television and digital texts, making it easier to quote, tweet, retweet, and memorize.

To conclude, 66 prepositions were identified in the Inaugurals Corpus, revealing four general usage patterns. First, a select few of 11 prepositions dominates the majority of occurrences. Second, a significant number of prepositions exhibit extremely low frequencies. Third, the preposition OF stands out with significantly higher scores, warranting its own category. Lastly, a group of eight prepositions has never been observed in the Inaugural Corpus. Furthermore, these patterns corroborate the findings of previous work on synchronic and diachronic data. The last remark concerns the preposition-to-word ratio. It has been observed that the frequency of prepositions has decreased over time, with one preposition occurring in every five words in 18th- and 19th-century addresses, compared to one in every eight words in the 21st century.

Analyzing preposition usage frequencies is just the beginning of a more in-depth investigation into their metaphorical usages and underlying conceptual basis. Chapter 6 will examine the metaphors and metonymies expressed via prepositions in greater detail.

References

Anthony, Laurence. 2022. *AntConc (Version 4.2.0) [Computer Software]*. https://www.laurenceanthony.net/software. Tokyo, Japan: Waseda University.

Biber, Douglas & Edward Finegan. 2001. Diachronic relations among speech-based and written registers in English. In Conrad, S. & Biber, Douglas (ed.), *Variation in English: Multi-dimensional studies*, 66–83. London, England: Longman.

Bird, Steven, Ewan Klein & Edward Loper. 2009. *Natural language processing with Python: Analyzing text with the natural language toolkit*. Sebastopol, CA: O'Reilly Media.

Carter, Ronald & Michael McCarthy. 2006. *Cambridge grammar of English: A comprehensive guide spoken and written English grammar and usage*. Cambridge, England: Cambridge University Press.

Charteris-Black, Jonathan. 2004. Metaphor in American presidential speeches. In *Corpus approaches to critical metaphor analysis*, 87–110. New York, NY: Palgrave MacMillan.

Geeraerts, Dirk. 2010. The doctor and the semantician. *Quantitative Methods in Cognitive Semantics: Corpus-driven Approaches*. Walter de Gruyter 46. 63.

Gibbs, Raymond W. 2011. Evaluating conceptual metaphor theory. *Discourse Processes* 48(8). 529–562.

Heylighen, Francis & Jean-Marc Dewaele. 1999. *Formality of language: Definition, measurement and behavioral determinants*. [Internal Report, Center Leo Apostel, Free University of Brussels].

Hudson, Richard. 1994. About 37% of word-tokens are nouns. *Language* 70(2). 331–339.

Johansson, Stig & Knut Hofland. 1989. *Frequency analysis of English vocabulary and grammar: Based on the LOB corpus*. Oxford, England: Clarendon Press.

Leech, Geoffrey, Paul Rayson & others. 2001. *Word frequencies in written and spoken English: Based on the British National Corpus*. New York, NY: Routledge.

Lewis, Craig M. & Francesco Grossetti. 2022. A statistical approach for optimal topic model identification. *The Journal of Machine Learning Research*. JMLRORG 23(1). 2553–2572.

Lim, Elvin T. 2002. Five trends in presidential rhetoric: An analysis of rhetoric from George Washington to Bill Clinton. *Presidential Studies Quarterly*. Wiley Online Library 32(2). 328–348.

Mindt, Dieter & Christel Weber. 1989. Prepositions in American and British English. *World Englishes* 8(2). 229–238.

Rissanen, Matti, Merja Kyto, Merja Kytö & Minna Palander-Collin. 1993. *Early English in the computer age: Explorations through the Helsinki Corpus*. Berlin, Germany: Mouton de Gruyter.

Rowley, Christina. 2010. *An intertextual analysis of Vietnam War films and US presidential speeches*. [Doctoral dissertation, University of Bristol, Bristol].

Samuels, Robert. 2008. Auto-modernity after postmodernism: Autonomy and automation in culture, technology, and education. In McPherson, Tara, John, D. & MacArthur, Catherine T. (ed.), *Digital youth, innovation, and the unexpected*, 219–240. Cambridge, MA: The MIT Press.

Semino, Elena. 2017. Corpus linguistics and metaphor. In Dancygier, B. (ed.), *The Cambridge handbook of cognitive linguistics*, 463–476. Cambridge, England: Cambridge University Press.

Wikberg, Kay. 2008. The role of corpus studies in metaphor research. In Johannesson, Nils-Lennart & Minugh, David (ed.), *Selected papers from the 2006 and 2007 Stockholm metaphor festivals*, 33–48. Stockholm, Sweden: Acta Universitatis Stockholmiensis.

Zhang, Weiwei, Dirk Geeraerts & Dirk Speelman. 2015. Visualizing onomasiological change: Diachronic variation in metonymic patterns for WOMAN in Chinese. *Cognitive Linguistics*. De Gruyter 26(2). 289–330.

6 Patterns of preposition-based conceptualization in inaugurals

6.1 Conceptual mappings of metaphor-related prepositions

Before delving into the analysis of conceptual mappings, it is essential to present some key figures regarding the metaphor-related prepositions extracted from the Inaugural Corpus.

Each occurrence of the prepositions in the corpus was studied within the sentences in which they were used according to the procedures outlined by the Pragglejaz Group (Steen et al. 2010). These procedures were applied to determine whether each preposition is used to convey a literal or metaphorical meaning. In the latter case, the preposition in question was categorized as a metaphor-related preposition. This analysis identified 630 instances where prepositions were used metaphorically. These metaphoric instances are going to be examined in terms of their source and target domains in the remainder of this section.

When considering their source domains, 32 domains were extracted from the metaphor-related prepositions in the Inaugural Corpus. Table 6.1 provides a comprehensive illustration of these domains, along with their corresponding frequency rates and percentages.

According to these rates, three key observations can be made. First, four source domains stand out with remarkably high frequencies: psychology, the human body, light, and motion.

The two most frequently occurring domains are primarily concerned with humans. By including other related domains such as life cycles, family, and community, we can create a comprehensive semantic field that encompasses a broad spectrum of biological, psychological, and social aspects of human existence. When considering percentages, these combined domains account for 29.31%. Furthermore, by combining the domains of motion and roads under the label of a journey, a score of 12.48% is attained. Thus, they become the second most frequent semantic field. Likewise, the domains of light and darkness make up 10.89% when combined. In summary, by combining source domains that share thematic similarities into semantic fields, three frequent fields emerge: human beings, journeys, and light/darkness. The

DOI: 10.4324/9781003369646-6

Table 6.1 The source domains of the extracted metaphor-related prepositions

	Domains	Count	Percentage (%)		Domains	Count	Percentage (%)
1	Psychology	49	9.70	17	Time	11	2.18
2	Human body	48	9.50	18	Weather	9	1.78
3	Light	39	7.72	19	Religion	8	1.58
4	Motion	34	6.73	20	Community	7	1.39
5	Communication	33	6.53	21	Music	7	1.39
6	Roads	29	5.74	22	Agriculture	7	1.39
7	Life cycles	27	5.35	23	Container	7	1.39
8	Building	24	4.75	24	Nature	6	1.19
9	Objects	21	4.16	25	Machines	6	1.19
10	Family	17	3.37	26	Poverty	6	1.19
11	Diseases	16	3.17	27	Verticality	5	0.99
12	Darkness	16	3.17	28	Prison	4	0.79
13	War	16	3.17	29	Tribunal	3	0.59
14	Commerce	15	2.97	30	Food	3	0.59
15	Water	14	2.77	31	Size	2	0.40
16	Education	14	2.77	32	Heat	2	0.40

second observation pertains to the finding that most of these semantic fields include an underlying system, which may be either natural or mechanical in nature. When metaphor-related prepositions are employed within these fields, they serve as potent catalysts, bringing the systems' internal relationships to the forefront. These relationships are accentuated and used to structure abstract systems related to politics and ethics. The third and final observation is about the prepositions' geometrical dimensions of verticality and size. Their relatively low frequencies indicate that metaphor-related prepositions are primarily used to establish connections between entities, accentuating their image schematic functions while downplaying their geometric properties.

From the perspective of target domains, the nation/state and high principles stand out as the most frequent domains. As for the first domain, an additional search was conducted on the Inaugural Corpus using AntConc software to double-check the prevalence of the concept. The results revealed that the words "government" and "people" were particularly salient, ranking 28th and 29th in frequency out of a total of 9,096 words. Upon closer examination of the list, it becomes evident that "government" and "people" are outranked only by small particles such as articles, pronouns, prepositions, and quantifiers. More specifically, the word "government" appeared 604 times, and the term "people" appeared 596 times throughout the entire corpus. These high frequencies sound natural in a corpus where presidents are supposed to express their views and opinions on governments and the people who will be governed. In addition to "government", similar words such as "America", "country", "states", "nation", "republic", and "union" make a total of 2,052 raw occurrences in the Inaugural Corpus.

In the extracted metaphors, the nation/state is conceptualized in terms of various source domains, such as a person, a living organism, a family, a human body, a community, and a building.

In addition to the government, the term "people" received the second highest share of metaphorical representation. It appeared 596 times in the Inaugural Corpus. A similar term, "citizen(s)", occurred 304 times in the same corpus. When these two occurrences are combined, they confirm the importance of the people in a political system that relies on the ballot box. These two concepts are usually associated by means of metaphor-related prepositions, as in this memorable quote:

> 1 "And so, my fellow Americans: ask not what your country can do for you--ask what you can do for your country" (Kennedy 1961).

The preposition FOR establishes a connection between two entities: a country and its people in terms of a relationship between a benefactor and a beneficiary. President Kennedy redefined this relationship by introducing a new configuration. In the same vein, another quote follows the same reconfiguration strategy, but it has not received similar attention. Discussing the government's role, President Reagan defined the relationship between the government and the people by means of four prepositions.

> 2 "… it's not my intention to do away with government. It is rather to make it work; work *with* us, not *over* us; to stand *by* our side, not ride *on* our back [emphasis added]" (Reagan 1981)

These four metaphor-related prepositions represent four scenarios of the possible relationships between the government and the people.

The second target domain is high principles and, more precisely, freedom and justice. Their high frequency is indicative of their significance to American political culture. The concept of freedom, including the terms "free" and "liberty", appeared 495 times, and the terms "justice" and "just" appeared 138 and 73 times, respectively. Metaphor-related prepositions conceptualize these principles and similar abstract ideas in terms of a wide range of experiences such as commercial transactions, journeys, music, catching and fighting diseases, farming, light, and darkness.

Returning to the tendency of conceptual mapping across natural and mechanical systems, the following section will provide additional details and insights regarding this particular aspect.

6.2 System metaphors and cross-system mapping

As political metaphors are about the political system, they are conceptualized in terms of another system, whether natural or human-made. Cross-system mapping serves to coalesce both the principles and concepts of a political

Table 6.2 Systems and their source domains

Systems	Salient Source Domains
Biological system	Human body
Living organism	Life cycles
	Psychology
	Diseases
	Communication
Social organization	Family
	Community
Natural order	Weather
	Water
	Light
	Darkness
	Agriculture
Urban organization	Roads
	Building
	Commerce
Other systems	Music
	Time
	Objects

system with other systems and the inherent structure and relationships of these systems. Table 6.2 displays the major systems observed in the metaphors of OF.

The variety of systems indicates that political metaphors are in constant need of recruiting concepts and structures from concrete systems. For example, the biological system is recruited to underscore the intrinsic naturalness of the political system, thereby enhancing the credibility and rationality of its norms and values. The overall effect of intrinsicness "celebrates existing power relationships and makes them seem a normal and acceptable part of the natural order" (Gamson et al. 1992: 380). In this way, a cross-system mapping generates compelling political arguments, drawing from both biological fatalism and mechanical efficacy, in order to persuade the general public to embrace the political order as natural, effective, and legitimate. Diachronically speaking, natural systems were recruited to enhance metaphorical reasoning whenever there was a debate that questioned the political system. Such metaphors are deployed to defend its legitimacy. Illustrative examples of these debates can be found in the prominent topics of the 1800, 1860, and 2021 elections. Natural systems and their features of spontaneity, intrinsicness, and durability provide vital supporting arguments for presidents facing fears of a central government, doubts about the nature of the new political system, and even the horrors of a civil war.

Similarly, concepts from other systems, such as commercial transactions, roads, and travel, are used to frame the American presidents' perceptions of policies and future plans. For example, commerce-based metaphors are used to reason about concepts, such as peace, freedom, and citizenship, entailing that these ideals hold an inherent value akin to commodities and that political action is driven by economic gain and regulated by the will of the market. Commerce is a "self-regulating system" (Lyotard 1984: 12) that entails that society can readjust itself in case of any dysfunction. During the social unrest of the Civil Rights Era, metaphors based on self-regulating systems were widely used in order to propagate and encourage self-adjustment, confidence, and optimism.

Though metaphors drawn from other systems serve to simplify the complexities of a political system and achieve pragmatic functions, they have some risks. First, the cross-system mapping is likely to generate metaphors that reflect the president's construal rather than the political system itself. When a president describes the political system in terms of another system, this implies that he believes that the other system offers an accurate description and explanation of the issues at hand. In other words, the politician's description of a political situation is usually consistent with the inherent logic of the source system. For example, source domains underlying metaphors like "arm of our Government" (Polk 1845) and "rude hand of power" (Pierce 1853) can generate metaphors of wars that legitimize the use of force and even transgress laws and human rights. Second, as long as politicians keep recruiting conceptual experiences from other systems than politics, politics remains an open system that can be affected by other systems. Some source domains are drawn from systems that are incompatible with politics in their character and key features, yet they still motivate a wide range of political metaphors. A cross-system mapping implies either that the political system is unable to establish its own identity and arguments or that politicians are reluctant to disclose all the secrets of their system. Finally, relying on another system as a constant source domain may create a recurrent correspondence between that system and politics. While such recurrent correspondence can motivate conventional metaphors, it may also create "a tendency to inertia", as Dobuzinskis (1992: 368) put it. This inertia is likely to stagnate cross-system mapping and resist the dynamics of diachronic factors.

In addition to the conceptual basis of the metaphor-related prepositions, the inaugurals include instances of mixed metaphors. The next section describes and explains how prepositions mix with other parts of speech in their metaphorical extensions.

6.3 The coherence of metaphors

The inaugurals are not metaphorically homogeneous texts. This may sound evident as we do not expect a text to consist of a single preposition repeated over and over again. We also do not expect to use the same conceptual metaphor throughout a given text. Thus, this section will examine two patterns of mixed metaphors. In the first pattern, metaphor-related prepositions tend to occur with other prepositions in the same sentence. In the second pattern, preposition-based metaphors mix with other metaphors based on other parts of speech.

It has been observed that metaphor-related prepositions appear with other prepositions of the same type, even in the same sentence. The co-occurrence of these prepositions is constrained by two factors: first, the scores of use frequency and metaphor patterns. As for the first factor, the more frequent a preposition is, the more it tends to co-occur with other prepositions. For example, the preposition OF forms a central metaphorical unit around which other prepositions appear in the same sentence. These prepositions provide complementary information to the meaning of the OF construct. This pattern can be illustrated by the metaphor "fire of freedom", for example, when it attracted two other metaphor-related prepositions (IN and OF), as in the following quote:

> 3 "And as hope kindles hope, millions more will find it. By our efforts, we have lit a fire as well, a fire *in* the minds of men. It warms those who feel its power. It burns those who fight its progress. And one day this untamed fire *of* freedom will reach the darkest corners *of* our world [emphasis added]" (Bush 2005).

The same pattern can be identified in the following quote, where three metaphor-related prepositions complement the main metaphorical OF in "the will of the nation".

> 4 "The will *of* the nation, speaking *with* the voice *of* battle and *through* the amended Constitution [emphasis added]" (Garfield 1881).

The second factor that contributes to the formation of a cluster of metaphor-related prepositions is the metaphor pattern and, more precisely, the components of the conceptual identity and conceptual space. Entities defined by the preposition OF are likely to be located and assigned a direction. This pattern implies that the metaphorical OF tends to co-occur with IN and TO within coherent metaphorical scenes, as in the following quotes:

> 5 "That element lies *in* the heart *of* humanity [emphasis added]" (Coolidge 1925).
> 6 "If we do not turn the hearts *of* children *toward* knowledge and character, we will lose their gifts and undermine their idealism [emphasis added]" (Bush 2001).

Patterns of preposition-based conceptualization in inaugurals 65

The most recurrent example of a coherent metaphor cluster is the FROM-TO construct that evokes progress. Examples include quotes of this sort:

> 7 "their rapid progress *from* infancy *to* manhood [emphasis added]" (Harrison 1841).
> 8 "How far have we come in man's long pilgrimage *from* darkness *toward* the light? [emphasis added]" (Eisenhower 1953).

Furthermore, another coherent cluster of metaphor-related prepositions was used by President Bush. It includes three prepositions, namely TOWARD, THROUGH, and TO, and it appeared in the same order in two adjacent sentences, which makes a perfect illustration of metaphor coherence, parallelism, and "consistency effect" (Gentner et al. 2001: 215).

> 9 "Great nations of the world are moving *toward* democracy *through* the door *to* freedom. Men and women of the world move *toward* free markets *through* the door *to* prosperity [emphasis added]" (Bush 1989).

As for their rhetorical effect, a well-crafted blend of such prepositions usually gives birth to memorable quotes. For example, President Lincoln mixed OF, BY, and FOR to describe the relationships between the government and the people. This cluster inspired other presidents to use the same three prepositions and create their own clusters.

> 10 "that government by an elite group is superior to government *for, by,* and *of* the people [emphasis added]" (Reagan 1981).
> 11 "They gave to us a republic, a government *of* and *by* and *for* the people, entrusting each generation to keep safe our founding creed [emphasis added]" (Obama 2013).

As for the second type of coherence, metaphor-related prepositions are consistent with other research that found nearly the same source domains for metaphors expressed by other parts of speech. For example, metaphor-related prepositions share all the seven source domains identified by Charteris-Black (2004). They are ordered by their use frequency as follows: conflicts, journeys, buildings, fire and light, physical environment, religion, and body parts. However, there is a disagreement between the findings of this study and those of Charteris-Black (2004) in terms of use frequency. In metaphor-related prepositions, parts of the body are one of the most frequent source domains, but it occupies the last ranking in Charteris-Black (2004). Conflict, the first source domain in Charteris-Black's list, is not among the frequent concepts in metaphor-related prepositions. Instead, conflict is expressed by the preposition AGAINST, which appeared only 114 times in the Inaugural Corpus.

Though there is a difference only in the use frequency of the source domains, metaphor-related prepositions do not include the prepositions UP and DOWN. The low frequency of these two prepositions constitutes an unexpected finding because literature abounds with assertive claims about the centrality of these prepositions in any discourse on social or political hierarchy. This low frequency can be explained by the fact that advocating national cohesion is far more important than propagating hierarchy, as illustrated by the following quotes:

> 12 "But in our seeking for economic and political progress as a nation, we all go up, or else we all go down, as one people" (Roosevelt 1937).

Similarly, President Clinton was openly critical of these divisive stratifications in the following quote:

> 13. "Powerful people maneuver for position and worry endlessly about who is in and who is out, who is up and who is down" (Clinton 1993).

It is interesting to note that UP and DOWN belong to the marginalized set, with UP being used 68 times while DOWN being used only 27 times in the Inaugural Corpus. In these occurrences, UP and DOWN are used more as adverbs than prepositions. The low frequency of prepositions of verticality leads to a corresponding scarcity of metaphors like HIGH STATUS IS UP, and LOW STATUS IS DOWN. The same applies to metaphors related to FRONT-BACK, UP-DOWN, and CENTER-PERIPHERY image schemas. The scarcity of these metaphors can be attributed to the inclination towards fostering inclusive discourse and discouraging stigmatization and segregation.

It has been shown that metaphor-related prepositions mix well with each other even in a single sentence, and they also mix well with metaphors expressed by other parts of speech. In terms of image schemas, the coherence of metaphors and metonymies could be attributed to the "schematic integrations", as stated by Mandler and Cánovas (2014: 528). The overall effect is coherence rather than a "clash of metaphorical imagery" (Kimmel 2010: 97).

6.4 Prepositions and their metonymic basis

The high frequency of the preposition OF suggests that metaphor-related prepositions are much more than merely conceptualizing nonspatial entities in terms of spatial ones as described in the literature. The preposition OF is not based on any spatial basis, yet it structures a wealth of metaphors in the corpus. Thus, it will be studied as a typical example of how metaphor-related prepositions are based on metonymies.

Patterns of preposition-based conceptualization in inaugurals 67

The linguistic metaphors of this preposition are built on the PART-WHOLE image schema and formulated according to the X of Y pattern in which X is a part, and Y is the whole to which X belongs. As it stands, this construction is a typical metonymy and, more precisely, a synecdoche. However, it is also metaphorical because it is based on a mapping between a concrete domain and an abstract one. Let us take a sample quote from the Inaugural Corpus to understand the components and stages of the conceptual mapping of the metaphorical OF. The quote reads as follows:

14 "Returning to the bosom of my country after a painful separation from it for ten years" (Adams 1797).

At this stage, the focus is only on the phrase "the bosom of my country". As shown in Table 6.3, the arrows refer to the conceptual mapping between the two domains and the two meanings of the preposition OF.

The last cells of Table 6.3 indicate a conceptual correspondence between two domains leading to the COUNTRY IS A HUMAN BODY metaphor. However, this metaphor appears to jump to conclusions, disregarding the intricacies that exist between the components of the conceptual domains, as illustrated in the first three cells. In other words, the phrase "the bosom of my country" involves more than a correspondence between two conceptual domains. Instead, the relational profile evoked by the preposition OF should not be disregarded. This preposition relates a concrete PART to an abstract WHOLE according to the following construction: A CONCRETE PART OF AN ABSTRACT WHOLE. More precisely, the mapping yields the following inference: the relationship between a real bosom of a real person is analogous to the relationship between an imaginary bosom and a country. This metaphorical relationship applies to all the linguistic metaphors in which the preposition OF relates a

Table 6.3 The conceptual mappings of President Adams's quote

Target Domain	Description		Description	Source Domain
the bosom	an abstract part of a country	↔	a concrete part of a body	the bosom
OF	a projected intrinsic relationship	↔	a naturally intrinsic relationship	OF
my country	an abstract whole	↔	a concrete whole	a human body
		↔	a concrete part of a person	a human body
a country	an abstract whole	↔	a concrete whole	a person

concrete domain with an abstract one. Tentatively, the figurative meaning is attained through the following stages and assumptions:

- First, a concrete PART implies the existence of a concrete WHOLE. For example, a bosom is one of the parts of a whole, which is a body. Thus, it implies the existence of a human body as a concrete whole to which the bosom belongs.
- Second, the concrete WHOLE is omitted but still implied. The word "body" does not appear in the phrase "the bosom of my country".
- Third, the concrete PART evokes a source domain. The concept of a bosom is the concrete item in the phrase, and it, therefore, suggests that its whole, the human body, is the source domain.
- Fourth, the abstract WHOLE evokes a target domain. The abstractness of the concept of a country makes it a perfect candidate to be a target domain.
- Fifth, the abstract WHOLE is transformed into a dividable entity analogous to the concrete WHOLE. As both entities lend themselves to division into parts, a specific part can be made salient.
- Sixth, the preposition OF establishes a relation between the PART and its WHOLE, creating a metonymic basis by which we access the WHOLE through its PART.
- Seventh, the concrete PART is mapped onto the imaginary PART. Naming is just one step of the conceptual mapping between these two PARTS. As the imaginary PART is abstract and invented, it acquires the relational profile of the concrete PART. The conceptual mapping consists of understanding the imaginary PART in terms of the concrete PART.

Phrases like "the bosom of my country" and their underlying pattern, A CONCRETE PART OF AN ABSTRACT WHOLE, are based on the preposition OF. Accordingly, trajectors can be conceptualized as intrinsically integrated into their landmarks. This view is in line with Langacker (2008a: 18), who studied the preposition OF and concluded that "the relationship between its trajector and landmark is somehow intrinsic rather than contingent". Intrinsicness projects the stability of both attributes and relations in the source domains onto the political system and its concepts. As the preposition OF reinforces intrinsicness, it presupposes that each component of a government is linked to the government in an intrinsic relationship in the same way human organs are integral parts of the body or a father is an intrinsic part of his family. The political system that presidents have repeatedly attempted to define and legitimize must look stable with permanent attributes and whose components are linked by long-lasting relationships.

In addition to intrinsicness, the metaphorical OF serves to convey durability, the very same feature that a reliable political system demands. The inevitable cycle of day and night; the predictable movement of water, seas, and oceans; and the unavoidable consequences of weather evoke the certainty of scientific truths and promote the durability of the laws. The preposition OF creates metaphorical relationships that reinforce one message; governments, like natural phenomena, are governed by irrevocable laws. Even history is reduced, by metaphors of light and darkness, to the natural rotation of day and night, as in the following quote:

> 15 "We have endured a long night of the American spirit. But as our eyes catch the dimness of the first rays of dawn" (Nixon 1969).

By naturalizing such metaphors, nonhuman, ahistorical, and durable rules regulate the historical and flexible concepts of human life.

From the perspective of metonymy, the pattern of A CONCRETE PART OF AN ABSTRACT WHOLE encompasses two metonymies. The first metonymy is primed by the concrete "bosom" and provides mental access to the conceptual domain of the human body. The second metonymy is primed by the abstract "bosom" and provides mental access to the conceptual domain of the state/nation. In the case of "the bosom of my country", there is an interaction between metaphor and metonymy. Barcelona (2003: 46) explains that metaphor is created because "the metonymically understood source structure is able to match the metonymically understood target structure". In this way, the conceptual metaphor of A NATION IS A HUMAN BODY is plausible, thanks to these two metonymies that underpin it. More specifically, the bosom of a country is a fictive concept invented owing to metaphorical and metonymic projections. It can also be interpreted as a (re)categorization that figurative language allows. Accordingly, language users employ metaphor and metonymy to create new categories that (re)describe reality. In the words of conceptual integration theory, new categories are generated in the form of an emergent blend. In the case of the bosom of the country, it is a hybrid concept, or "a hybrid conception, fictive in nature, combining selected features of each input space", as Langacker (2008b: 51) put it.

Like other prepositions, the metaphorical OF imposes its image-schematic constraints on the compatibility between the two conceptual domains. Accordingly, it makes the relational interpretation of "the bosom of my country" significantly richer compared to the reductionist cross-mapping. The relationships conveyed by OF are enriched through "structural similarity", as de Mendoza Ibáñez and Cervel (2023) suggest. As metaphor-related prepositions involve such rich conceptual processes, the notation system has to reflect the complexities inherent in these processes.

6.5 Conceptual notation revisited

A conceptual mapping of any metaphor usually involves two experiential domains where we perceive one domain in terms of another. However, in metaphor-related prepositions, these two domains are related and enriched by a preposition, and we cannot perceive one domain in terms of another without that preposition.

As the relationship between the two conceptual domains is semantically affected by the preposition in question, we suggest that this preposition should be included in any conceptual notation. It is essential to remember that a preposition creates a new relationship between two entities in a metaphor, and more importantly, it constrains that relationship. Given this important role, a proper notation system should refer to prepositions and not overlook their significance.

The common notation system neglects prepositions because most metaphor research takes nouns as the default part of speech to be used in conceptual metaphors. This tradition may be the outcome of the classic examples of metaphor in the literature, such as "Richard is a lion" and "Juliet is the sun". The notation of A is B is perfect for nominal metaphors because mapping is primarily a systematic correspondence between the attributes of two nouns by which we perceive the attributes of Richard in terms of the attributes of a lion. However, mapping in preposition-based metaphors is primarily a systematic correspondence between two relationships. For example, in a statement like "Jill is in poverty", we understand the situation in terms of the preposition IN because it is the particle that relates Jill with poverty. The schematic structure of IN constrains our understanding of Jill's situation in terms of a typical person situated in a concrete location. In this way, our construal of the situation is constrained and simultaneously structured by two mental spaces. While the first space has a typical person in a concrete location, the second space comprises Jill in a socioeconomic state. In terms of conceptual integration networks, the first space has the organizing frame through the preposition IN with its spatial configurations and functions. In a Simplex network, the first space is applied to the second by which a conceptual mapping is formulated as follows: THE RELATIONSHIP BETWEEN A PERSON AND THEIR SOCIOECONOMIC STATE IS THE RELATIONSHIP BETWEEN A PERSON AND THEIR CONCRETE LOCATION. As it stands, this conceptual metaphor may sound accurate and inclusive, but it is not concise and, thus, sounds awkward. What is required is a notation that neither reduces the mapping to the two conceptual domains nor neglects the preposition and its schematic meaning.

Metaphor-related prepositions necessitate a formula in which the preposition is as salient as in its original context. In response to this need, Nickels (2013: 126) suggests that metaphor-related prepositions be allotted the shorthand notation "Ap B" instead of A is B in order to emphasize the differences between a preposition-based mapping and a nominal two-domain mapping.

Nickels's proposal may be improved by replacing the generic letter "p" with the specific preposition that represents the intended relationship between concepts A and B. By incorporating this modification, the revised formula would be as follows: A [PREPOSITION] B. For example, the new formula will read as follows: A IN B, A ON B, and A OF B.

References

Adams, John. 1797. First Inaugural Address. *The American Presidency Project*. https://www.presidency.ucsb.edu/documents/inaugural-address-18 (24 January, 2017).

Barcelona, Antonio. 2003. On the plausibility of claiming a metonymic motivation for conceptual metaphor. In Barcelona, Antonio (ed.), *Metaphor and metonymy at the crossroads: A cognitive perspective*, 31–58. Berlin, Germany: Mouton de Gruyter.

Bush, George. 1989. First Inaugural Address. *The American Presidency Project*. https://www.presidency.ucsb.edu/documents/inaugural-address (24 March, 2022).

Bush, George W. 2001. First Inaugural Address. *The American Presidency Project*. https://www.presidency.ucsb.edu/documents/inaugural-address-52 (24 January, 2017).

Bush, George W. 2005. Second Inaugural Address. *The American Presidency Project*. https://www.presidency.ucsb.edu/documents/inaugural-address-13 (24 January, 2017).

Charteris-Black, Jonathan. 2004. *Corpus approaches to critical metaphor analysis*. 1st edn. New York, NY: Palgrave MacMillan.

Clinton, William J. 1993. First Inaugural Address. *The American Presidency Project*. https://www.presidency.ucsb.edu/documents/inaugural-address-51 (24 January, 2017).

Coolidge, Calvin. 1925. First Inaugural Address. *The American Presidency Project*. https://www.presidency.ucsb.edu/documents/inaugural-address-50 (24 January, 2017).

de Mendoza Ibáñez, Francisco José Ruiz & Mari'a Sandra Peña Cervel. 2023. Structural similarity in figurative language: A preliminary cognitive analysis. *Lingua*. Elsevier 290. 1–20.

Dobuzinskis, Laurent. 1992. Modernist and postmodernist metaphors of the policy process: Control and stability vs. chaos and reflexive understanding. *Policy Sciences* 25. 355–380.

Eisenhower, Dwight D. 1953. First Inaugural Address. *The American Presidency Project*. https://www.presidency.ucsb.edu/documents/inaugural-address-3 (24 January, 2017).

Gamson, William A., David Croteau, William Hoynes & Theodore Sasson. 1992. Media images and the social construction of reality. *Annual Review of Sociology* 18. 373–393.

Garfield, James. 1881. First Inaugural Address. *The American Presidency Project*. https://www.presidency.ucsb.edu/documents/inaugural-address-39 (24 January, 2017).

Gentner, Dedre, Brian Bowdle, Phillip Wolff & Consuelo Boronat. 2001. Metaphor is like analogy. In Gentner, Dedre, Holyoak, Keith J. & Kokinov, Boicho N. (ed.), *The analogical mind: Perspectives from cognitive science*, 199–253. Cambridge, MA: MIT Press.

Harrison, William Henry. 1841. First Inaugural Address. *The American Presidency Project*. https://www.presidency.ucsb.edu/documents/inaugural-address-29 (24 January, 2017).

Kennedy, John F. 1961. First Inaugural Address. *The American Presidency Project*. https://www.presidency.ucsb.edu/documents/inaugural-address-2 (24 January, 2017).

Kimmel, Michael. 2010. Why we mix metaphors (and mix them well): Discourse coherence, conceptual metaphor, and beyond. *Journal of Pragmatics*. Elsevier 42(1). 97–115.

Langacker, Ronald W. 2008a. The relevance of cognitive grammar for language pedagogy. In Knop, Sabine De & Rycker, Teun De (ed.), *Cognitive approaches to pedagogical grammar*, 7–35. Berlin, Germany: Mouton de Gruyter.

Langacker, Ronald W. 2008b. *Cognitive grammar: A basic introduction*. Oxford, England: Oxford University Press.

Lyotard, Jean-Francois. 1984. *The postmodern condition: A report on knowledge*. Manchester, England: Manchester University Press.
Mandler, Jean M. & Cristóbal Pagán Cánovas. 2014. On defining image schemas. *Language and Cognition* 6(4). 510–532.
Nickels, Edelmira L. 2013. *Metaphors in congressional discourse: Cognitive frames of the political status of Puerto Rico*. [Doctoral dissertation, Indiana University].
Nixon, Richard. 1969. First Inaugural Address. *The American Presidency Project.* https://www.presidency.ucsb.edu/documents/inaugural-address-1 (24 January, 2022).
Obama, Barack. 2013. Second Inaugural Address. *The American Presidency Project.* https://www.presidency.ucsb.edu/documents/inaugural-address-15 (24 January, 2017).
Pierce, Franklin. 1853. First Inaugural Address. *The American Presidency Project.* https://www.presidency.ucsb.edu/documents/inaugural-address-32 (24 January, 2017).
Polk, James K. 1845. First Inaugural Address. *The American Presidency Project.* https://www.presidency.ucsb.edu/documents/inaugural-address-30 (24 January, 2017).
Reagan, Ronald. 1981. First Inaugural Address. *The American Presidency Project.* https://www.presidency.ucsb.edu/documents/inaugural-address-11 (24 January, 2017).
Roosevelt, Franklin D. 1937. Second Inaugural Address. *The American Presidency Project.* https://www.presidency.ucsb.edu/documents/inaugural-address-7 (24 January, 2022).
Steen, Gerard J., Aletta G. Dorst, J. Berenike Herrmann, Anna Kaal, Tina Krennmayr & Trijntje Pasma. 2010. *A method for linguistic metaphor identification: From MIP to MIPVU*. Amsterdam, The Netherlands: John Benjamins Publishing.

7 Cognitive functions of metaphor-related prepositions in political narratives

7.1 The cognitive model: an overview

Presidents communicate their representations to their audience through coherent narratives that reflect and affect how political thoughts and contemporary issues are conceptualized. These narratives are built on metaphors as "conventionalized systems of reasoning" (Gentner et al. 2001: 241) that establish a pattern of understanding and reasoning about political concepts and actions. As "the very purpose of our perceptual and cognitive mechanisms is to provide a representation of this reality" (Evans & Green 2006: 48), metaphors and metonymies are supposed to represent reality in a coherent and consistent manner.

Within this framework, metaphor-related prepositions extracted from the Inaugural Corpus are supposed to provide coherent representations of political reality. To illustrate this point, this tentative model describes how such prepositions are systematically used to conceptualize political concepts and action through two processes: conceptual identity and conceptual space. In the first process, some prepositions specify the identity of political concepts by highlighting a particular identifying feature. The second process includes prepositions that locate political concepts and actions in a conceptual space within three distinct frames of reference: location, direction, and extent.

In the sections that follow, each process will be described in terms of its constituent prepositions, their conceptual domains along with diachronic variations. Before examining both processes in more detail, it is essential to know which prepositions are included in each process. The conceptual identity involves prepositions such as OF, WITH, LIKE, AS, FOR, and BY, while the conceptual space includes IN, INTO, FROM, TO, ON, AT, OFF, TOWARD, and TOWARDS.

7.2 Conceptual identity

Politics is notorious for being a complex field in terms of its ideas and actions. Part of this complexity lies in the challenge of offering accessible definitions and descriptions of these concepts. In this regard, the relational profile of the

DOI: 10.4324/9781003369646-7

metaphor-related prepositions serves to create and communicate a conceptual image of political concepts such as the state, the nation, presidential power, and the exercise of political authority over the people.

OF may be considered a typical preposition that stands for conceptual identity. In its metaphorical senses, this preposition takes advantage of its PART-WHOLE image schema and its metonymic structure to define and characterize the identity of almost all the abstract concepts in politics. Accordingly, a salient attribute is created and emphasized to act as a defining and restrictive referential factor (Merle 2017: 5). From the perspective of the PART-WHOLE image schema, one specific PART is made so salient and distinctive that it becomes able to define and refer to the WHOLE.

In its conceptualization of the identity of political concepts, the preposition OF relies on many source domains such as the parts of the body, living organisms, family, education, light/darkness, building, acoustics, commerce, objects, and other miscellaneous domains.

To start with body parts, a conceptual identity is evoked through metaphors based on A BODY PART-OF-CONCEPT construct, as in the following quotes:

1 "the bosom of my country" (Adams 1797).
2 "no rude hand of power or tyrannical passion is laid upon him with impunity" (Pierce 1853).
3 "The eyes of all nations are fixed on our Republic" (Jackson 1833).

The nation/state in (1)–(3) is conceptualized as a body and accessed through one of its organs. What is more interesting is the preference of some parts of the body over others. For example, "arm" was used only once, while "heart" appeared 17 times in the Inaugural Corpus. One likely explanation is that the arm is typically associated with force and conveys negative connotations incompatible with the image of presidents in democracies. On the other hand, the "heart", as the traditional locus of emotions and knowledge, has retained its saliency throughout the history of American inaugurals. As for the "hand", it was used 16 times in the Inaugural Corpus. Its saliency is likely to reside in its function of control and possession. American presidents use this body part to specify in whose hands political power rests.

Likewise, the features of a living organism contribute to the definition of the concept of a nation.

The mapping between a nation and a living organism is explained in its biological, mental, and spiritual dimensions. The human life cycle, prime years, health, and life itself are all mapped on the stages of the nation's growth, as in the following quotes:

4 "The life of a Nation is the fullness of the measure of its will to live" (Roosevelt 1941).
5 "youthful vigor of the country" (Monroe 1817).

The inferences of (4) and (5) revolve around the well-being of the nation. Just as humans are prone to grow physically strong during their prime years, presidents define the nation's strength in terms of human physical prowess.

Family, as a source domain, has usually been activated to characterize the concept of a nation. By highlighting their nation's conceptual identity in terms of a family, presidents are more likely to be concerned with their country's unity and cohesion. The family-based identity is demonstrated by the recurrent use of the phrase "father of our country". The father's concept can also be traced to the Scriptures and the Holy Father figure. Trim (2018: 5) explains that the French monarchy, before the French Revolution, used to refer to the king as the father of his subjects. Another family-related term is family itself. It is used mainly to define the identity of the international community in terms of the "family of nations" (Buchanan 1857; Garfield 1881; McKinley 1901; Wilson 1917). As family ties bind its members, the international community cherishes similar bonds.

Besides, light and darkness are used as defining features of specific identities. The metaphors of light are used to define the regimes that endorse democratic ideals, while those of darkness are used to define undemocratic regimes. President Washington's original phrase "fire of liberty" was frequently cited by subsequent presidents whenever it was vital to rekindle the democratic spirit of their nation.

Furthermore, a conceptual identity of a nation is profiled by means of metaphors drawn from buildings and construction, as in the following quotes:

6 "we recognize the earliest and firmest pillars of the Republic" (van Buren 1837).
7 "the Constitution, which is the cement of the Union" (Madison 1809).

The metaphorical OF serves to emphasize that a sound foundation is an integral part of the conceptual identity of the nation.

In addition to buildings, a conceptual identity is profiled from the domain of acoustics. Based on our shared knowledge of sounds and music, the preposition OF permits mapping "via the sense of hearing" (Trim 2011: 13). Different auditory constituents relate to their respective wholes, as in the following quote:

8 "the voice of the nation" (Jefferson 1801).

In general, voice integrates nature and law, as explained by Rousseau via the emotion of natural compassion, which "in a state of nature supplies the place of laws, morals, and virtues, with the advantage that none are tempted to disobey its gentle voice" (as cited in Derrida 1997: 173). Early American presidents usually portray themselves in a natural relationship with their country, listening to its gentle voice and obeying its calls.

Value is another feature of the conceptual identity of various entities. The metaphorical OF highlights components such as price, cost, and value as intrinsic parts of certain abstract concepts such as peace and liberty. Examples of value include the following quotes:

> 9 "We are called to meet the price of our liberty" (Cleveland 1885).
> 10 "the price of this peace" (Eisenhower 1957).

These principles are highly cherished in American culture and provide a basis for the "valuable commodity metaphor", as Kövecses (2000: 106) suggests.

Moreover, a conceptual identity can be structured by natural phenomena, including four natural source domains: weather, landscape, water, and plants. For example, tempests highlight the identity of negatively evaluated concepts, such as political change, while water highlights positively evaluated concepts, such as peace, as in the following quotes:

> 11 "No nation, however old or great, escapes this *tempest* of change and turmoil" (Eisenhower 1957).
> 12 "the still *waters* of peace" (Obama 2009).

Having considered the preposition OF, it is essential to investigate how other prepositions contribute to the characterization of abstract entities in the corpus. FROM identifies a concept through one of its salient ingredients, as in the following quote:

> 13 "happiness springs from a perfect equality of political rights" (van Buren 1837).

Various similar abstract concepts are defined in terms of their sources, such as national pride, confidence, and faith.

Likewise, the metaphorical WITH contributes to the conceptual image of the nation and other abstract entities. This preposition relates a trajector and a landmark "as elements of an overall ensemble", as explained by Lindstromberg (2010: 214). The assembly of a trajector with the content of its landmark creates a new image of the trajector, as in the following quote:

> 14 "the flag that waves above and that fills our hearts with pride" (Obama 2013).

Conceptual identities defined by metaphor-related prepositions include various legal, moral, social, and political concepts. Defining the identity of these concepts is what makes the presidents in charge of teaching their people the conceptual identity of their nation and the shared political concepts via a set of coherent metaphor-related prepositions.

Having explained what is meant by a conceptual identity and how metaphor-related prepositions are used in such conceptualizations, the next section discusses the second process, which is the conceptual space.

7.3 Conceptual space

Metaphor-related prepositions characterize abstract concepts and actions by locating them in a conceptual space. These entities can be in both static and dynamic states, but they vary in their conceptual mappings and diachronic saliency. If we take the concept of the nation as a sample entity, the conceptual space answers three questions: (1) where is the nation? (2) where is it heading? and (3) how far has it progressed? The answers to these questions inform us about an abstract entity's location, the direction of its motion, and the extent of its progress, respectively. A more detailed account of these three representations (direction, location, and extent) is provided in the following subsections.

7.3.1 Location

Within the conceptual space, metaphor-related prepositions locate various abstract entities relative to their respective landmarks. These landmarks, which are originally not physical locations, are turned into locations, thanks to the schematic relations of the prepositions that precede them.

A recurrent landmark is evoked through various body parts. For example, the phrase "in hands" is used to refer to the possessor of power in the political system with an emphasis on the location of that power. Hands act as a relative reference frame according to which power is located, as in the following quote:

15 "The Government has been in the hands of the people" (Monroe 1817).

As a metonymy, "hands" act as a PART and stand for holding power and locate it in the WHOLE, which is the people. When conceptualized as a location, human hands may function as a container giving rise to inferences pertaining to possession and control. Additionally, location is usually associated with accountability for that power. Thus, when power is located in one's hands, its exercise remains under their responsibility. Presidents Lincoln and Kennedy used the same phrase "in your hands" to specify the location and highlight the interface between space and accountability.

16 "In your hands, my dissatisfied fellow-countrymen, and not in mine, is the momentous issue of civil war" (Lincoln 1861).
17 "In your hands, my fellow citizens, more than mine, will rest the final success or failure of our course" (Kennedy 1961).

Diachronically speaking, these quotes are separated by a span of a century, yet they use the same preposition to evoke the same conceptual space with the same inferences. In a political system built on caution of excessive power in one branch of government, presidents are more likely to assert that the ultimate power is located in the hands of the people, the ultimate source of power and legitimacy.

In addition to "the hands of the people", the phrase "the hand of God" is used to remind the audience of the chain of locations and control, particularly in the last few sentences of most American inaugurals. In politics, humans relentlessly compete for power, seeking to grasp it within their hands. However, beyond the confines of politics, the hands of the Almighty God hold the ultimate reins of power, unchallenged and unmatched by any competition.

Another location conceptualized in body parts is the human heart. It functions as a figurative location, functioning as the locus of moral values, intellect, political convictions, and certain specific emotions such as sympathy.

18 "Whoever would understand in his heart the meaning of America will find it in the life of Abraham Lincoln" (Reagan 1981).
19 "its existence only awakens in my heart a deeper sympathy for those who have to bear it or suffer from it" (Taft 1909).
20 "he told of his dream that one day America would rise up and treat all its citizens as equals before the law and in the heart" (Clinton 1997).

Taken together, these metaphorical landmarks can be grouped under the heading of the national heart. More specifically, this heart is the locus of shared knowledge, as President Reagan put it:

21 "In our hearts, we know what matters" (Reagan 1981).

In addition to body parts, darkness was conceptualized as a location in the following quote:

22 "seeking Divine guidance to help us each and every one to give light to them that sit in darkness" (Roosevelt 1937).

Herriot (2008: 65) explains that this figurative location is linked to its original text: the Bible, precisely Psalm 107. As a location, metaphorical darkness highlights how unpleasant the current location is and urges the location holders to relocate to a better location.

When emotions are conceptualized as abstract locations, they are mainly related to axiological evaluations. Positive emotions, generated by harmony and dignity, are associated with American democratic principles and policies.

23 "With which shall we be most likely to live in harmony and friendly intercourse?" (Jefferson 1805).

Cognitive functions of metaphor-related prepositions   79

Negative emotions refer to undemocratic regimes and unpopular policies. For example, "in hopelessness" is related to "tyranny", and "in fear" is linked to undemocratic governments.

> 24 "those who live today in fear under their own governments" (Truman 1949).

Furthermore, socioeconomic conditions are stigmatized for particular social groups inside the U.S.

> 25 "twilight years were spent in poverty" (Obama 2013).
> 26 "Mothers and children trapped in poverty" (Trump 2017).

These conditions are characterized by poverty and portrayed as locations that confine their inhabitants. In-groups and out-groups were characterized by the space they occupy, and their identities are constructed via spatial prepositions. The focus on mothers and children may be contextualized within the postmodern paradigm in which marginalized and voiceless groups are awarded more privileges than in the modernist model of metaphor.

Another set of locations is expressed by the metaphorical ON. This location is structured by the SUPPORT image schema according to which a particular landmark acts as a location and, simultaneously, a supporting foundation to its trajector.

> 27 "our America, the America builded [sic] on the foundation laid by the inspired fathers, can be a party to no permanent military alliance" (Harding 1921).

The interplay of location and support serves to locate trajectors and, at the same time, to highlight the role of their landmarks as supporting foundations. In this way, conceptual location is not merely a mirror of spatial localization but also an added value generated by the function of support on which the existence of the trajectors rests. These metaphors derive their positive weight from both the supposedly solid foundations and the assumed verticality of the whole structure. In the inaugurals, most landmarks are shared moral values and political principles, adding prominence and credibility to their trajectors.

7.3.2 *Direction*

Within the frame of conceptual space, some metaphor-related prepositions are used primarily to inform about the direction of abstract entities. The high frequency of such metaphors can be explained by the fact that "people simulate motion even when motion is metaphorical" (Matlock 2012: 482). American presidents set the motion of their nation and consider giving directions to their people their core and sacred duty. The following quote explicitly describes the president's moral duty:

> 28 "I assume the solemn obligation of leading the American people forward along the road over which they have chosen to advance" (Roosevelt 1937).

The frequent use of direction prepositions is supported by the modernist theory that postulates a natural telos towards which human acts inevitably move. In other terms, these prepositions reflect "a cognitive bias toward dynamism", according to Talmy (2000: 171).

To emphasize the purposiveness of their plans, presidents systematically employ prepositions denoting directions. It is not surprising that a set of dynamic and directional prepositions such as TO, TOWARD, FOR, and INTO are used in their metaphorical senses to promote the purposes presidents intend to achieve. These prepositions relate policies with their goals in such a way that political agendas are conceptualized in terms of trajectors moving in the direction of goals. In practical terms, politicians take advantage of some metaphor-related prepositions to blend a prolonged cognitive state stretching from the current state to a better one in the future. Recurring goals include democracy, peace, prosperity, happiness, and freedom.

Setting goals has been an essential part of the representation of the nation. As early as 1801, President Jefferson set three fundamental goals in terms of destinations and a metaphorical road leading to them. This scene of a conceptual direction is based on the preposition TO, as illustrated in the following quote:

> 29 "let us hasten to retrace our steps and to regain the road which alone leads to peace, liberty, and safety" (Jefferson 1801).

In (29), President Jefferson enacts the role of the rational and efficient policy planner who can offer "guidance or steering for the purpose of achieving intended conditions or reaching a desired goal", as Dobuzinskis (1992: 357) put it.

Not only does conceptual direction highlight goals, but it also invokes concepts of improvement and hope. Metaphors of GOAL are, therefore, more likely to sustain a mood of hope by reinforcing the impression that the president is leading the country towards a better future. By combining hope with paths leading to goals, metaphor-related prepositions blend goals with positive motion verbs and emotion-related words. The blend consists of these four concepts and elements: (1) a goal offers "an inferential conceptualization of the entire path" (Ungerer & Schmid 2006: 224); (2) it is the future that counts; (3) there is hope; and (4) somebody is moving, of their own volition, towards the goal. This blend is manifest in the following samples:

30 "Men and women of the world move toward free markets through the door to prosperity" (Bush 1989).
31 "In a world moving toward liberty" (Bush 2005).

Although metaphor-related prepositions are based on the SOURCE-PATH-GOAL image schema, not all these components are equally significant. "We are generally more concerned with the goal of a motion event than with its source", Radden and Dirven (2007: 311) argue. The metaphors extracted from the Inaugural Corpus show that the SOURCE and PATH are less frequent than the GOAL. This asymmetry between prepositions of goal and those of the source and or the path is a reflection of "the goal-over-source principle" (Dirven & Verspoor 2004: 85) or "the goal bias principle" (Stefanowitsch 2018; Stefanowitsch & Rohde 2004). These principles frequently manifest in the Inaugural Corpus, particularly when the attainment of goals is conceptualized as a journey towards greater heights and a higher standard.

32 "Sometimes we will be rising toward the heights" (Roosevelt 1945).
33 "we invite the world to the same heights" (Harding 1921).

It is not surprising that presidents would opt for such an inspiring direction. The vertical direction has always been metaphorically associated with high status and well-being. Diachronically speaking, these goals kept appearing in reaction to temporary events such as the years of economic depression and the two World Wars. Conceptual direction persisted even during peace. From a metamodernist perspective, politicians need to set goals even if they know they can never be fulfilled.

34 "follow the same precise path to happiness" (Obama 2013).

These unfulfilled goals are usually expressed through figurative language, which reduces the responsibility burden when politicians fail to achieve these goals. It seems that politicians are aware that "people are not really going toward a natural but unknown goal, but they pretend they do so that they progress morally as well as politically", as Vermeulen and Van den Akker (2010: 5) reformulated Kant's negative idealism.

7.3.3 Extent

As part of the conceptual space, extent combines location and direction, but it emphasizes the amount of progress achieved. It is mainly evoked by the FROM-TO-construction and viewed from a "maximal scope" (Langacker 2008: 63–65). Its scope is maximal because the entire frame is portrayed, not just a part of it.

Within this entire frame, two main source domains, namely the life cycle and that of day and night, are recruited to communicate the metaphors of extent. The inherent natural evolution of these two cycles is activated to structure the advancement of political and social actions. The metaphorical FROM-TO-construction profiles political and social progress in terms of either growth from infancy to manhood or natural evolution from darkness to light.

> 35 "their rapid progress from infancy to manhood" (Harrison 1841).
> 36 "How far have we come in man's long pilgrimage from darkness toward the light?" (Eisenhower 1953).

In (35)–(36), prominence is placed on the amount of progress by juxtaposing the initial stage with the current one in such a way that progress becomes salient.

Linguistic metaphors that contain notions of light and darkness are often associated with the GOODNESS AS LIGHT and EVIL AS DARKNESS metaphors. However, the meanings of the prepositions involved in such metaphors give rise to the concept of extent in addition to the conceptual mapping between these domains. To conceptualize extent, the prepositions FROM and TO convey a process of gradual transformation culminating in achieved progress, as advocated by President Nixon:

> 37 "We have endured a long night of the American spirit. But as our eyes catch the dimness of the first rays of dawn, let us not curse the remaining dark. Let us gather the light" (Nixon 1969).

In addition to the prepositions FROM and TO, the preposition OFF is also used in metaphors of extent. It evokes "separation from (the surface of) a supporting Landmark", according to Lindstromberg (2010: 55). This meaning is exploited to highlight separation as the initial stage of progress. The extent of progress becomes more marked with landmarks such as poverty, earlier losses, and history.

> 38 "We must face a condition of grim reality, charge off our losses and start afresh" (Harding 1921).
> 39 "we offer a special pledge ... to assist free men and free governments in casting off the chains of poverty" (Kennedy 1961).

In (38) and (39), progress is evoked through moving from poverty to well-being or from the past to the present. In terms of their source domains, they are presented as a release from control, liberation from confinement, and forceful freedom from imprisonment.

Extent is also expressed by the preposition INTO, especially when it appears in a MOTION VERB-INTO construction.

40 "we led our beloved land into a new century" (Clinton 1997).
41 "... and turned the tide of history away from totalitarian darkness and into the warm sunlight of human freedom" (Reagan 1985).

Though the initial stage is sometimes absent, it is still implied, and the extent of the progress is emphasized.

Thus far, a tentative cognitive model has been presented to illustrate how metaphor-related prepositions are coherently and consistently used to represent political concepts and actions in terms of their conceptual identity and space (direction, location, and extent). Prepositions assume this role as they create relationships between a trajector and its landmark in which the latter is perceived as "the entity construed as being located, evaluated or described" (Langacker 2008: 81). Similarly, this tentative model accords with Joronen (2016: 97), who asserts that ontology "takes place topologically, i.e. it is place-bound". Metaphor-related prepositions have proven useful in addressing ontological questions by navigating through the conceptual space. This model is also consistent with the findings of Chilton (2004: 201–205), who specifies that "spatial metaphors make concepts of the group and identity available".

While Joronen and Chilton's models are limited to spatial prepositions, this study proves that the preposition OF holds exceptional significance in both its frequency of use and metaphorical applications. Moreover, this tentative model expands our understanding of how metaphor-related prepositions intricately shape our conceptualization of political concepts and actions.

References

Adams, John. 1797. First Inaugural Address. *The American Presidency Project*. https://www.presidency.ucsb.edu/documents/inaugural-address-18 (24 January, 2017).
Buchanan, James. 1857. First Inaugural Address. *The American Presidency Project*. https://www.presidency.ucsb.edu/documents/inaugural-address-33 (24 January, 2017).
Bush, George. 1989. First Inaugural Address. *The American Presidency Project*. https://www.presidency.ucsb.edu/documents/inaugural-address (24 March, 2022).
Bush, George W. 2005. Second Inaugural Address. *The American Presidency Project*. https://www.presidency.ucsb.edu/documents/inaugural-address-13 (24 January, 2017).
Chilton, Paul. 2004. *Analysing political discourse: Theory and practice*. 1st edn. London, England: Routledge.
Cleveland, Grover. 1885. First Inaugural Address. *The American Presidency Project*. https://www.presidency.ucsb.edu/documents/inaugural-address-40 (24 January, 2017).
Clinton, William J. 1997. Second Inaugural Address. *The American Presidency Project*. https://www.presidency.ucsb.edu/documents/inaugural-address-12 (24 January, 2017).
Derrida, Jacques. 1997. *Of grammatology*. Baltimore, MD: The Johns Hopkins University Press.
Dirven, René and Verspoor, Marjolyn (eds.). 2004. *Cognitive exploration of language and linguistics*. Vol. 1. Amsterdam, The Netherlands: John Benjamins Publishing.

Dobuzinskis, Laurent. 1992. Modernist and postmodernist metaphors of the policy process: Control and stability vs. chaos and reflexive understanding. *Policy Sciences* 25. 355–380.
Eisenhower, Dwight D. 1953. First Inaugural Address. *The American Presidency Project.* https://www.presidency.ucsb.edu/documents/inaugural-address-3 (24 January, 2017).
Eisenhower, Dwight D. 1957. Second Inaugural Address. *The American Presidency Project.* https://www.presidency.ucsb.edu/documents/second-inaugural-address (24 January, 2017).
Evans, Vyvyan & Melanie Green. 2006. *Cognitive linguistics: An introduction.* 1st edn. Edinburgh, Scotland: Edinburgh University Press.
Garfield, James. 1881. First Inaugural Address. *The American Presidency Project.* https://www.presidency.ucsb.edu/documents/inaugural-address-39 (24 January, 2017).
Gentner, Dedre, Brian Bowdle, Phillip Wolff & Consuelo Boronat. 2001. Metaphor is like analogy. In Gentner, Dedre, Holyoak, Keith J. & Kokinov, Boicho N. (ed.), *The analogical mind: Perspectives from cognitive science*, 199–253. Cambridge, MA: MIT Press.
Harding, Warren G. 1921. First Inaugural Address. *The American Presidency Project.* https://www.presidency.ucsb.edu/documents/inaugural-address-49 (24 January, 2017).
Harrison, William Henry. 1841. First Inaugural Address. *The American Presidency Project.* https://www.presidency.ucsb.edu/documents/inaugural-address-29 (24 January, 2017).
Herriot, Peter. 2008. *Religious fundamentalism: Global, local and personal.* London, England: Routledge.
Jackson, Andrew. 1833. Second Inaugural Address. *The American Presidency Project.* https://www.presidency.ucsb.edu/documents/inaugural-address-27 (24 January, 2017).
Jefferson, Thomas. 1801. First Inaugural Address. *The American Presidency Project.* https://www.presidency.ucsb.edu/documents/inaugural-address-19 (24 March, 2022).
Jefferson, Thomas. 1805. Second Inaugural Address. *The American Presidency Project.* https://www.presidency.ucsb.edu/documents/inaugural-address-20 (24 January, 2017).
Joronen, Mikko. 2016. Politics of being-related: On onto-topologies and "coming events." *Geografiska Annaler: Series B: Human Geography.* Wiley Online Library 98(2). 97–107.
Kennedy, John F. 1961. First Inaugural Address. *The American Presidency Project.* https://www.presidency.ucsb.edu/documents/inaugural-address-2 (24 January, 2017).
Kövecses, Zoltán. 2000. *Metaphor and emotion: Language, culture, and body in human feeling.* 2nd edn. Cambridge, England: Cambridge University Press.
Langacker, Ronald W. 2008. *Cognitive grammar: A basic introduction.* Oxford, England: Oxford University Press.
Lincoln, Abraham. 1861. First Inaugural Address. *The American Presidency Project.* https://www.presidency.ucsb.edu/documents/inaugural-address-34 (24 January, 2017).
Lindstromberg, Seth. 2010. *English prepositions explained.* Revised. Amsterdam, The Netherlands: John Benjamins Publishing.
Madison, James. 1809. First Inaugural Address. *The American Presidency Project.* https://www.presidency.ucsb.edu/documents/inaugural-address-21 (24 January, 2017).
Matlock, Teenie. 2012. Framing political messages with grammar and metaphor. How something is said may be as important as what is said. *American Scientist* 100. 478–483.

McKinley, William. 1901. Second Inaugural Address. *The American Presidency Project*. https://www.presidency.ucsb.edu/documents/inaugural-address-44 (24 January, 2017).
Merle, Jean-Marie. 2017. Les prépositions en contexte. Approche de la théorie des opérations prédicatives et énonciatives (TOPE). *Corela* HS-(22). 1–12.
Monroe, James. 1817. First Inaugural Address. *The American Presidency Project*. https://www.presidency.ucsb.edu/documents/inaugural-address-23 (24 January, 2017).
Murphy, Gregory Leo. 1996. On metaphoric representation. *Cognition* 60(2). 173–204.
Nixon, Richard. 1969. First Inaugural Address. *The American Presidency Project*. https://www.presidency.ucsb.edu/documents/inaugural-address-1 (24 January, 2022).
Obama, Barack. 2009. First Inaugural Address. *The American Presidency Project*. https://www.presidency.ucsb.edu/documents/inaugural-address-5 (24 January, 2022).
Obama, Barack. 2013. Second Inaugural Address. *The American Presidency Project*. https://www.presidency.ucsb.edu/documents/inaugural-address-15 (24 January, 2017).
Pierce, Franklin. 1853. First Inaugural Address. *The American Presidency Project*. https://www.presidency.ucsb.edu/documents/inaugural-address-32 (24 January, 2017).
Radden, Günter & René Dirven. 2007. *Cognitive English grammar*. Vol. 2. Amsterdam, The Netherlands: John Benjamins Publishing.
Reagan, Ronald. 1981. First Inaugural Address. *The American Presidency Project*. https://www.presidency.ucsb.edu/documents/inaugural-address-11 (24 January, 2017).
Reagan, Ronald. 1985. Second Inaugural Address. *The American Presidency Project*. https://www.presidency.ucsb.edu/documents/inaugural-address-10 (24 January, 2017).
Roosevelt, Franklin D. 1937. Second Inaugural Address. *The American Presidency Project*. https://www.presidency.ucsb.edu/documents/inaugural-address-7 (24 January, 2022).
Roosevelt, Franklin D. 1941. Third Inaugural Address. *The American Presidency Project*. https://www.presidency.ucsb.edu/documents/third-inaugural-address (24 January, 2017).
Roosevelt, Franklin D. 1945. Fourth Inaugural Address. *The American Presidency Project*. https://www.presidency.ucsb.edu/documents/inaugural-address-6 (24 January, 2017).
Stefanowitsch, Anatol. 2018. The goal bias revisited: A collostructional approach. *Yearbook of the German Cognitive Linguistics Association* 6(1). 143–166.
Stefanowitsch, Anatol & Ada Rohde. 2004. The goal bias in the encoding of motion events. In Radden, Günter & Panther, Klaus-Uwe (ed.), *Studies in linguistic motivation*, 249–267. Berlin, Germany/New York, NY: Mouton de Gruyter.
Taft, William Howard. 1909. First Inaugural Address. *The American Presidency Project*. https://www.presidency.ucsb.edu/documents/inaugural-address-46 (24 January, 2017).
Talmy, Leonard. 2000. Fictive motion in language and "ception." In *Language and space*, vol. 1, 99–175. Cambridge, The UK: The MIT Press.
Trim, Richard. 2011. *Metaphor and the historical evolution of conceptual mapping*. Basingstoke, England: Palgrave Macmillan.
Trim, Richard. 2018. Le pouvoir rhétorique de la métaphore famille dans les discours présidentiels américains et français. In Trim, Richard & Kudszus, Winfried (ed.), *Métaphores de l'austérité et austérité des métaphores : Metaphors of austerity & the austerity of metaphors*, 87–99. Paris, France: Editions L'Harmattan.
Truman, Harry S. 1949. First Inaugural Address. *The American Presidency Project*. https://www.presidency.ucsb.edu/documents/inaugural-address-4 (24 January, 2017).
Trump, Donald J. 2017. First Inaugural Address. *The American Presidency Project*. https://www.presidency.ucsb.edu/documents/inaugural-address-14 (24 January, 2017).

Ungerer, Friedrich & Hans-Jorg Schmid. 2006. *An introduction to cognitive linguistics*. Harlow, England: Pearson Education Limited.
van Buren, Martin van. 1837. First Inaugural Address. *The American Presidency Project*. https://www.presidency.ucsb.edu/documents/inaugural-address-16 (24 January, 2017).
Vermeulen, Timotheus & Robin Van den Akker. 2010. Notes on metamodernism. *Journal of Aesthetics & Culture* 2(1). 1–14.
Wilson, Woodrow. 1917. Second Inaugural Address. *The American Presidency Project*. https://www.presidency.ucsb.edu/documents/inaugural-address-48 (24 January, 2017).

8 Tracing patterns of diachronic variations across the inaugurals

8.1 Metaphor variations

This section examines the evolution of metaphor-related prepositions from a diachronic perspective. The American historical timeline starts with the Federalist Era (1789–1800). During this era, metaphor-related prepositions were mainly used to conceptualize the nature of the new political system and its underlying principles, liberty and justice. These conceptualizations reflect the debate between the Federalists and the Anti-Federalists and the impact of the Constitution's principles on the political system. Presidents Washington and Adams used source domains related to the parts of the body, living organisms, light, communication, and water to formulate metaphors based on the image schemas of the metaphorical OF and BY. Examples of such metaphors include "voice of my country", "guided by no lights", "fire of liberty" (Washington 1789, 1793), and "happiness of the nation" (Adams 1797).

The Jeffersonian Democracy (1801–1816) and its emphasis on limited government had a significant impact on the variation of metaphor-related prepositions. The presidents of this period did not conceptualize good governments as natural organisms. Thus, they did not embrace the STATE AS A PERSON metaphor and its entailments. Instead, they valued good governments in terms of the goals that they promised to achieve. The concepts of path and road, such as in the "path of justice" (Jefferson 1805), first appeared during this period. Similar metaphors built on the image schema of TO were also emphasized, such as "the road which alone leads to peace, liberty, and safety" (Jefferson 1801).

It is interesting to note that the Federalist and Jeffersonian Eras witnessed the highest rates of metaphor-related prepositions, as shown in Figure 8.1.

The next era, the Era of Good Feelings (1817–1828), was full of positive emotions but not with many metaphor-related prepositions. The low frequencies can be explained by the reconciliation policy adopted by the presidents of this era. Prepositions were used in metaphors based on correspondences between the emotional well-being of a person and the strength of a nation, such as "youthful vigor of the country" (Monroe 1817), "happiness of our country" (Monroe 1821), and "the opinions and feelings

DOI: 10.4324/9781003369646-8

88 Tracing patterns of diachronic variations across the inaugurals

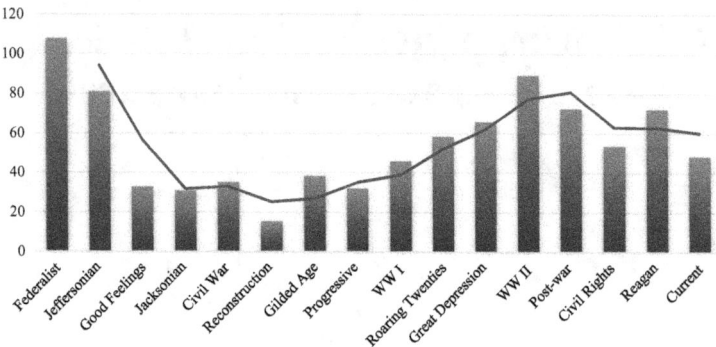

Figure 8.1 The normalized frequencies of all metaphor-related prepositions in the Inaugural Corpus.

of our country" (Adams 1825). Negative feelings caused by party tensions and political rivalries were condemned through metaphors based on undesired plants, such as "weed of party strife" (Adams 1825).

The Jacksonian Era (1829–1848) had an equally low frequency of metaphor-related prepositions, even though most presidents of that era rehearsed the republican ideals that originated in the Jeffersonian Era. The republican political system was conceptualized in terms of human biology, family, life cycles, and buildings. These source domains draw the frame of a government with natural structure, inevitable growth, and solid foundations. Typical metaphorical expressions of this era include "we recognize the earliest and firmest pillars of the Republic" (van Buren 1837), "progress from infancy to manhood" (Harrison 1841), "the strong protecting arm of our Government" (Polk 1845), and "family of free and independent States" (Polk 1845).

During the Civil War Era (1849–1864), the presidents were preoccupied with the threats to the nation's union. Consequently, the presidents of that era frequently employed the term "the father of the country" (Buchanan 1857; Pierce 1853; Taylor 1849) to refer to and honor President Washington as the icon of national unity. Similarly, prepositions were used in metaphors emphasizing national unity, such as "chorus of the Union" and "In your hands, my dissatisfied fellow-countrymen and not in mine, is the momentous issue of civil war" (Lincoln 1861).

The metaphors of the Reconstruction Era (1965–1880) were the lowest across the inaugurals' history. The political situation was precarious and uncertain, leading presidents to be cautious in expressing their views on the nature and power of the central government and the status of the Southern States. Instead, they were more assertive regarding the social conditions in the Southern States. The term "poverty" was introduced into the Inaugural Corpus for the first time in the phrase "the ten States in poverty" (Grant 1869).

The preposition IN was first used to conceptualize a socioeconomic state in terms of a physical location.

The usage of metaphor-related prepositions rose again in the Gilded Age (1881–1896). Body parts were utterly absent from the list of the source domains, and so were state, nation, and government from the list of the target domains. Instead, there was a remarkable frequency of PATH OF ABSTRACT CONCEPT construct as in "the avenues of hope" (Harrison 1889) and "the paths of civilization and education" (Cleveland 1893). Likewise, President Cleveland's criticism of partisan practices was evoked by metaphors based on repulsive source domains such as diseases, heat, and noise, as in "the heat of the partisan" (Cleveland 1885), "symptom of insidious infirmity" (Cleveland 1893), and "the din of party strife" (Cleveland 1893).

The presidents of the Progressive Era (1897–1916) were committed to reform and modernization initiatives. Thus, they used body-based metaphors to underscore the inherent naturalness of their reforms. Prepositions were used in metaphors such as "in the hands of the Federal Executive" (Taft 1909), "the hands of Democrats" (Wilson 1913), and "an eye single to the standards of justice and fair play" (Wilson 1913). These new policies were not without costs. Similarly, prepositions were useful in weight-based metaphors aimed at mitigating the burden of income tax, as in "men and women and children upon whom the dead weight and burden of it all has fallen" (Wilson 1913).

The next historical period is World War I (1917–1920), in which President Wilson devoted almost all his address to justifying his country's involvement in the war. Prepositions like OUTSIDE and UPON were used in metaphors aimed at evading responsibility, as in "matters lying outside our own life as a nation" (Wilson 1917) and "matters have more and more forced themselves upon our attention" (Wilson 1917). Consequently, Americans "have drawn us more and more irresistibly into their own current and influence" (Wilson 1917). President Wilson also recruited family and its obligations to justify his political commitments towards "the family of nations" (Wilson 1917). The whole address follows the same style: metaphor-related prepositions, among other rhetorical and stylistic tools, were used to legitimize his war policy and defend his decision against the prevailing pacific and pro-neutrality mood of the era. One of his arguments is that wars can strengthen national unity: "We are being forged into a new unity amidst the fires" (Wilson 1917). President Wilson's address has a higher frequency of metaphor-related prepositions than his predecessors. This high frequency can be partially explained by the new style of presidents talking directly to the larger public, known as the "rhetorical presidency".

The impact of World War I can be felt throughout the 1921 address in which the term "civilization" was used 21 times. It was an attempt by President Harding to persuade the "lost generation" of the Roaring Twenties (1921–1928) that the U.S. had preserved its civilization in comparison with the nations that had destroyed theirs during the war. Civilization was conceptualized in terms of different concrete concepts such as roads, living organisms, and teaching, such as in "It is the oldest lesson of civilization" (Harding 1921), "the gaze of all civilization" (Harding 1921), and "the path of civilization" (Coolidge 1925). Likewise, the metaphorical phrase "the heart of America" (Harding 1921) first appeared in this era, as well as other similar phrases such as "the will of America" (Harding 1921) and "the mind of America" (Coolidge 1925), drawing on conceptual mappings between the psychological well-being of human beings and the strength of a nation.

Metaphors of the Great Depression Era (1929–1940) involve two types. The first describes the current situation, while the second offers solutions. In the first type, darkness, as a source domain, was recruited to describe the current situation via metaphor-related prepositions such as "in every dark hour of our national life" (Roosevelt 1933) and "sit in darkness" (Roosevelt 1937). In addition to darkness, conceptual domains based on diseases were invoked to structure metaphors such as "cancers of injustice" (Roosevelt 1937). These metaphors reflect the harsh reality of the economic recession and its social repercussions. The second type of metaphor that advocates hope and progress was built on conceptual mappings from paint, roads, motion, and verticality. These metaphors aimed at promoting an economic plan as promising as the New Deal. Examples of metaphors include "progress to higher standards" (Hoover 1929), "progress toward prosperity" (Hoover 1929), "they are moving toward stronger moral and spiritual life" (Hoover 1929), and "It is not in despair that I paint you that picture" (Roosevelt 1937).

The exceptional circumstances of World War II (1941–1948) prompted the emergence of metaphors based on animals, personification, and verticality. The preposition AS was used in the following simile: "we must live as men, not as ostriches, nor as dogs in the manger" (Roosevelt 1945). The animal metaphor was meant to champion courage and noble conduct during the war. Similarly, the preposition LIKE was used in three consecutive similes to conceptualize the country as a person "A nation, like a person, has a body", "A nation, like a person, has a mind", and "A nation, like a person, has something deeper" (Roosevelt 1941).

The President's argument is built on the conviction that the survival of a nation is analogous to the survival of a person. As for verticality, the preposition TOWARD was used in the following metaphor: "we will be rising toward the heights" (Roosevelt 1945). The preposition was meant to convey a purposeful upward movement towards a direction laden with a positive evaluation. These three source domains work together to evoke patriotic feelings within the audience, particularly during these challenging times.

The social unrest at home and the Cold War abroad had an immediate impact on the conceptual mappings of the Post-War Era (1949–1968). The most frequent and distinctive mapping of the period relies on the source domains of light, darkness, and prison. In terms of the target domains, freedom stands out as the most frequent concept. The preposition IN was used to conceptualize freedom as an abstract location, according to Truman (1949): "live in freedom". This location, laden with a positive evaluation, was juxtaposed with the contrasting location "live today in fear" (Truman 1949). The freedom-advocating metaphors were highly frequent in President Eisenhower's addresses. One noteworthy example is President Washington's famous expression, "the sacred fire of liberty", which Eisenhower (1957) reformulated as "the light of freedom". Additionally, President Eisenhower used the metaphorical OF to create other metaphors conveying his support for freedom and political reform, including "shackles of the past" (Eisenhower 1953), "weight of fear", "winds of change", "tempest of change", and "shoulders of mankind" (Eisenhower 1957).

The Civil Rights Era (1969–1980) had its own challenges, which affected the choice of conceptual domains. The concepts of the previous era, such as freedom, peace, and dignity, were all replaced by metaphors that evoke "a crisis of the spirit", to borrow President Nixon's words. Within this crisis, "America has suffered from a fever of words" (Nixon 1969). In this era, Americans "endured a long night of the American spirit" (Nixon 1969). Drawing from diseases, natural disasters, and buildings, metaphor-related prepositions of this era portray an image of America different from that of the victorious country fully proud of its achievements in World War II and its new role as a model and preacher for peace and democracy. Metaphors of this era include "the valley of turmoil" (Nixon 1969), "the cup of despair" (Nixon 1969), "walls of hostility" (Nixon 1973), and "bridges of understanding" (Nixon 1973). It is interesting to note that the metaphorical VOICE-OF construct usually evokes positive concepts and positive evaluations, such as "the voice of my country" (Nixon 1969; Washington 1789, 1793), "voice of experience" (Harrison 1889), and "voices of freedom" (Roosevelt 1941). However, this same construct was not as positive in this era as it used to be. For example, social activists were conceived as "the voices of quiet anguish" (Nixon 1969). In fact, President Nixon was well aware of the rhetorical power of the VOICE-OF construct, and he accentuated its positive connotations and emotional appeal to urge the conflicting factions to listen to "the voices of the heart" (Nixon 1969). In addition to the metaphorical OF and voice-based conceptualizations, light and darkness were recruited as source domains to frame the Civil Rights Era's social unrest as in "We have endured a long night of the American spirit. But as our eyes catch the dimness of the first rays of dawn" (Nixon 1969). These arguments are intended to convey reassurance and hope by establishing conceptual mappings between social issues and the natural cycle of day and night. Daylight consistently disperses the darkness of the night. In general, metaphors of this era advocate hope by directing the people's attention to "the dawn of a new age" (Nixon 1973).

The Age of Reagan (1981–2008) was characterized by an optimistic and forward-looking outlook. This attitude was manifest in the prevailing motion metaphors expressed through prepositions like TO, TOWARD, and INTO, and a wide range of motion verbs, such as walk, march, move, and progress. These motion metaphors highlight particular destinations such as liberty, justice, progress, and democracy. Examples of these metaphors include phrases like "journey of progress and justice" (Bush 2005), "In a world moving toward liberty" (Bush 2005), "the road to an America rich in dignity" (Reagan 1985), and "moving toward democracy" (Bush 1989).

A frequent variation of these motion metaphors is built on the THROUGH-THE-DOOR-TO construct, structured by the PATH image schema, such as "through the door to prosperity" and "through the door to freedom" (Bush 1989). In addition to goals, freedom was commonly conceptualized as a valuable commodity during this era. This conceptual mapping makes the commodity's price a salient feature, as in "The price for this freedom at times has been high, but we have never been unwilling to pay that price" (Reagan 1981). The term 'freedom' was remarkably used in both the 1989 and 2005 addresses, making 21, 58% of all its occurrences in the Inaugural Corpus. The first address coincided with the freedom movements in the Eastern Bloc, while the second address reflected the post-9/11 policy. Furthermore, light and darkness remained salient source domains throughout the Age of Reagan. They are used in positive self-representation and negative representation of other undemocratic regimes, as in "this untamed fire of freedom will reach the darkest corners of our world" (Bush 2005). The blend of light with the concept of freedom is as old as the American inaugurals themselves. President Washington's original phrase, "the sacred fire of liberty", was either quoted or reformulated whenever the concept of freedom was at stake. In this era, this same blend between light and freedom is evoked by "sunlight" in the 1985 address, "sunshine" in the 1993 address, "flame" in the 1997 address, and "untamed fire" in the 2005 address.

The Current Era (2009–2021) comprises the addresses of only three presidents, but it is still accumulating its distinctive features. As they stand now, the metaphors in these addresses do not reflect the Era's main concerns, except for their emphasis on poverty as a bounded location. Instead, they rehearse the American culture's traditional themes, such as deference to President Washington as the father of the nation, promotion of freedom as a light, dissemination of happiness and prosperity as paths, and propagation of peace as a natural phenomenon. Typical examples of metaphors of this era include "rising tides of prosperity and the still waters of peace" (Obama 2009), "path to happiness" (Obama 2013), and "precious light of freedom" (Obama 2013).

To sum up, each era can be represented by a quote that includes a metaphor-related preposition, serving as a summary of the political and socioeconomic climate that influenced the generation of the metaphor. Table 8.1 illustrates these representative quotes along with the names of the presidents who uttered them, organized according to their historical periods.

Each era in American history has its own context that prompted its own metaphors. The selected quotes capture the essence of each era and provide insight into the prevailing sentiment of the time. However, they do not distinguish between replicated metaphors and those that emerge as novel and

Table 8.1 Historical eras and their representative metaphor

Era	Representative Quote	President
The Federalist Era (1789–1800)	"the voice of my country" "fire of liberty"	(Washington 1789, 1793)
The Jeffersonian Era (1801–1816)	"path of justice"	(Jefferson 1805)
The Era of Good Feelings (1817–1828)	"happiness of our country"	(Monroe 1821)
The Jacksonian Era (1829–1848)	"the strong protecting arm of our Government"	(Polk 1845)
The Civil War Era (1849–1864)	"the chorus of the Union"	(Lincoln 1861)
The Reconstruction Era (1965–1880)	"the ten States in poverty"	(Grant 1869)
The Gilded Age (1881–1896)	"the din of party strife"	(Cleveland 1885)
The Progressive Era (1897–1916)	"in the hand of private interests"	(Wilson 1913)
The World War I (1917–1920)	"the family of nations"	(Wilson 1917)
The Roaring Twenties (1921–1928)	"the path of civilization"	(Coolidge 1925)
The Great Depression Era (1929–1940)	"progress toward prosperity" "in every dark hour of our national life"	(Hoover 1929) (Roosevelt 1933)
The World War II Era (1941–1948)	"the life of a nation" "we will be rising toward the heights"	(Roosevelt 1941) (Roosevelt 1945)
The Post-War Era (1949–1968)	"the light of freedom" "the winds of change"	(Eisenhower 1957) (Eisenhower 1957)
The Civil Rights Era (1969–1980)	"a long night of the American spirit"	(Nixon 1969)
The Reagan Age (1981–2008)	"the road to an America rich in dignity" "this untamed fire of freedom"	(Reagan 1985) (Bush 2005)
The Current Era (2009–2021)	"path to happiness"	(Obama 2013)

unique. The forthcoming section seeks to identify the factors that contributed to the metaphors' variations.

8.2 Patterns of diachronic variations

The most significant remark is that metaphor-related prepositions oscillate between stability and change. "The inaugural must ensure continuity, but must also promise change" (Hinckley 1990: 22). Likewise, Mieder (2001: 169) affirms that American inaugural addresses "are meant to be timely and timeless". As shown in Section 8.1, some source and target domains have kept reappearing, and, at the same time, some new ones emerged at certain times and then disappeared. The most likely explanation is that there are factors of stability and change that affect the behavior of the conceptual mapping of the prepositions in question. These factors will be further analyzed in Sections 8.2.1 and 8.2.2.

8.2.1   Factors of diachronic stability

Long-term patterns are shaped by five stabilizing factors. The first stabilizing factor is related to prepositions themselves. As a closed group, there is little or no chance of coining new prepositions. Instead, the same set of prepositions is constantly and continuously used. Trim (2011: 35) argues that "the different structures in a language can have a certain amount of influence, albeit limited, on conceptual mapping". Though its limited impact, this syntactic factor stabilizes the conceptual mapping of metaphor-related prepositions. The second factor that contributes to the stability of metaphorical patterns is the semantics of the English prepositions. Most of the prepositions' meanings have not undergone any significant changes, at least in the historical period of the inaugurals. These meanings are highly affected by stable patterns of their respective image schemas. In this way, the intrinsic relations of the preposition OF and the schematic relations of the rest of the prepositions make conceptual mapping stable. Third, most metaphors expressed by prepositions rely on conventional conceptual mapping in which source domains emphasize stability and durability. These semantic fields explain the prevalence of order-related metaphors. For example, natural and human-made order include human biology and psychology or natural phenomena; social organizations such as family, community, and commerce; and human activities such as music, building, and farming. These systems provide coherent and relevant concepts that suit a "consensual rhetorical discourse" (Meyer 2010: 415). By relying on conventional intersystem mapping, political metaphors establish "a tendency to inertia" (Dobuzinskis 1992: 368), by which conceptual mappings remain constant. The fourth factor is related to the impact of "conceptual-cognitive context" (Kövecses 2015, 2020). Accordingly, metaphors are primed by the common metaphorical conceptual system, ideology, knowledge about past events, and interests and concerns. In other words, American presidents have constantly embraced the major tenets of the shared political culture. Consequently, they keep using metaphors that "comply with officially declared principles of USA", as Kubát and Cech (2016: 23) put it. A stable conceptual mapping, which propagates timeless and shared political ideals, contributes to political consensus and societal coherence. As American presidents have to rehearse these common concepts in their speeches, they usually rely on the same conceptual source domains for their metaphors, resulting in a greater degree of stability. The fifth and final factor deals with the inaugurals' generic properties and their impact on the stability of conceptual mappings.

Presidential inaugurals form a well-established genre with its own structure, norms, themes, and specifications. For example, the inaugurals have been taking place in nearly the same "communication situation" since their inception (Schaffner 1997: 3). Preserving these generic properties is a vital aspect of safeguarding the national political culture. This view is supported by Campbell and Jamieson (1990: 21), who assert that American presidents "must affirm that they will transmit the institution intact to their successors". In terms of metaphor choices, preserving these generic properties entails using the same conceptual mappings, leading to consistent and enduring conceptual stability.

These five factors combined tend to produce stable mappings that generate conventional metaphors. Once conventionalized, metaphors tend to be saved in "lexical storage" (Gentner et al. 2001: 216). As American presidents usually rehearse shared values in their addresses, they tend to repeat conventional metaphors retrieved from that lexical storage. However, it would be simplistic to claim that all the inaugurals are identical, ignoring all factors of change.

8.2.2   Factors of diachronic change

The change factors imply the existence of metaphor variations without contradicting the factors of stability listed above. While the latter explains the replication of conventional metaphors, the former explains the creation of novel metaphors.

Novel metaphors are affected by five factors of change. First, changes in the relationship between American presidents and their people have had an impact on the presidential discourse and, more specifically, the creation of new metaphors. This relationship evolved from a constitutional presidency to a party presidency and eventually to a rhetorical presidency, with each phase dictating its distinctive conceptual mapping. For example, the constitutional presidency is "grounded in the formal institutional arrangements of the constitutional text" (Broughton 2009: 167), while during the period of the party presidency, presidents expressed their "fidelity to the parties" (Korzi 2004: 40). Modern presidents portray themselves as "protectors and defenders of the people" (Lim 2002: 339). Each phase has its own salient concepts, which entail crafting distinct metaphors. The second factor is the relational potential of the prepositions themselves. This potential resides in their reparameterization function, through which prepositions introduce new parameters or redefine the existing ones, giving rise to fresh conceptualizations (Lapaire 2017: 14). Although they are a closed group, prepositions have a remarkable capacity to generate an unlimited number of relationships. They can connect an infinite number of trajectors to an infinite number of landmarks. Any novel metaphor is likely to include creative usages of prepositions that take advantage of their relational profile and their inherent potential for fresh reconfigurations. The third factor of change is the president's idiosyncratic style and character. Though presidents typically review past inaugural addresses, they often deliver speeches that mirror their own unique style and personality. The findings of this study do not demonstrate that the first inaugural has served as a template for other presidents to replicate its metaphor-related prepositions. Many metaphor-related prepositions used by President Washington could not survive for a long time, while new conceptual mappings appeared in the course of history. Like all politicians, American presidents have "the passion for distinction", as President Adams put it, and they, therefore, craft distinct metaphors. Distinction implies meeting the rhetorical challenge, which, in its turn, requires creating new metaphors as "a sign of genius", as Aristotle put it. The fourth factor deals with the influence of cultural and historical circumstances on the emergence of metaphors. This factor invokes the role of context in prompting specific metaphors to meet the demands of specific discourse situations. For example, historical events offer incentives for the emergence of novel metaphors. Trim (2011) argues that "single historical events may cause salience in particular items to increase considerably over a short period of time". For example, the first seven addresses (1789–1813) had the highest frequency of metaphor-related prepositions because this period witnessed an intense debate on the nature of the political system between the defenders of the central government and the defenders of more rights to the individual states. After this phase, there was a lengthy period, ranging from 1813 to 1909, in which the usage of metaphor-related prepositions fell sharply. During this period, the economic boom and party fidelity did not prompt any novel metaphors. However, the situation changed drastically during the 20th century. The main historical events, such as the two World Wars, the Great Depression, the Cold War, and the Civil Rights incidents, contributed to the rise of metaphor-related prepositions. The fifth and final factor of change is the impact of the paradigmatic shifts from modernity to postmodernism and eventually to contemporary post-postmodernism. Each paradigm imposed its values on conceptual mapping ranging from the modernist glorification of reason and progress, then to the postmodernist skepticism and glorification of diversity, and eventually to the emerging paradigm and its discourse of hope. In terms of source domains, religion, one of the metanarratives of modernity, has significantly diminished in its saliency as a source domain. In the meantime, most contemporary metaphors seem to favor economics and biology (Trim 2011: 182). In fact, paradigmatic shifts have affected not only conceptual mappings but also the nature of a political text. The latter developed from a scientific text to a critical text and eventually to a digimodernist text, which is "the outcome of a silent negotiation between viewer and screen" (Kirby 2009: 296).

The factors of stability and those of change represent two distinct frames. Within the stability frame, metaphors function as a tool to reinforce the hegemony of the dominant cognitive model and reinforce "the bounds of the accepted discourse" (Entman 1993: 55). However, in the change frame, metaphors serve as a tool to challenge the status quo and advocate for alternative perspectives.

References

Adams, John. 1797. First Inaugural Address. *The American Presidency Project.* https://www.presidency.ucsb.edu/documents/inaugural-address-18 (24 January, 2017).
Adams, John Quincy. 1825. First Inaugural Address. *The American Presidency Project.* https://www.presidency.ucsb.edu/documents/inaugural-address-25 (24 January, 2017).
Broughton, J. Richard. 2009. The inaugural address as constitutional statesmanship. *Quinnipiac Law Review* 28. 265–320.
Buchanan, James. 1857. First Inaugural Address. *The American Presidency Project.* https://www.presidency.ucsb.edu/documents/inaugural-address-33 (24 January, 2017).
Bush, George. 1989. First Inaugural Address. *The American Presidency Project.* https://www.presidency.ucsb.edu/documents/inaugural-address (24 March, 2022).
Bush, George W. 2005. Second Inaugural Address. *The American Presidency Project.* https://www.presidency.ucsb.edu/documents/inaugural-address-13 (24 January, 2017).
Campbell, Karlyn Kohrs & Kathleen Hall Jamieson. 1990. *Deeds done in words: Presidential rhetoric and the genres of governance.* Chicago, IL: The University of Chicago Press.
Cleveland, Grover. 1885. First Inaugural Address. *The American Presidency Project.* https://www.presidency.ucsb.edu/documents/inaugural-address-40 (24 January, 2017).
Cleveland, Grover. 1893. First Inaugural Address. *The American Presidency Project.* https://www.presidency.ucsb.edu/documents/inaugural-address-42 (24 January, 2017).
Coolidge, Calvin. 1925. First Inaugural Address. *The American Presidency Project.* https://www.presidency.ucsb.edu/documents/inaugural-address-50 (24 January, 2017).
Dobuzinskis, Laurent. 1992. Modernist and postmodernist metaphors of the policy process: Control and stability vs. chaos and reflexive understanding. *Policy Sciences* 25. 355–380.
Eisenhower, Dwight D. 1953. First Inaugural Address. *The American Presidency Project.* https://www.presidency.ucsb.edu/documents/inaugural-address-3 (24 January, 2017).
Eisenhower, Dwight D. 1957. Second Inaugural Address. *The American Presidency Project.* https://www.presidency.ucsb.edu/documents/second-inaugural-address (24 January, 2017).
Entman, Robert Mathew. 1993. Framing: Toward clarification of a fractured paradigm. *Journal of Communication* 43(4). 51–58.
Gentner, Dedre, Brian Bowdle, Phillip Wolff & Consuelo Boronat. 2001. Metaphor is like analogy. In Gentner, Dedre, Holyoak, Keith J. & Kokinov, Boicho N. (ed.), *The analogical mind: Perspectives from cognitive science*, 199–253. Cambridge, MA: MIT Press.
Grant, Ulysses S. 1869. First Inaugural Address. *The American Presidency Project.* https://www.presidency.ucsb.edu/documents/inaugural-address-36 (24 January, 2017).
Harding, Warren G. 1921. First Inaugural Address. *The American Presidency Project.* https://www.presidency.ucsb.edu/documents/inaugural-address-49 (24 January, 2017).
Harrison, Benjamin. 1889. First Inaugural Address. *The American Presidency Project.* https://www.presidency.ucsb.edu/documents/inaugural-address-41 (24 January, 2017).

Harrison, William Henry. 1841. First Inaugural Address. *The American Presidency Project.* https://www.presidency.ucsb.edu/documents/inaugural-address-29 (24 January, 2017).
Hinckley, Barbara. 1990. *The symbolic presidency: How presidents portray themselves.* New York, NY: Routledge.
Hoover, Herbert. 1929. First Inaugural Address. *The American Presidency Project.* https://www.presidency.ucsb.edu/documents/inaugural-address-9 (24 January, 2017).
Jefferson, Thomas. 1801. First Inaugural Address. *The American Presidency Project.* https://www.presidency.ucsb.edu/documents/inaugural-address-19 (24 March, 2022).
Jefferson, Thomas. 1805. Second Inaugural Address. *The American Presidency Project.* https://www.presidency.ucsb.edu/documents/inaugural-address-20 (24 January, 2017).
Kirby, Alan. 2009. *Digimodernism: How new technologies dismantle the postmodern and reconfigure our culture.* London, England: Continuum.
Korzi, Michael J. 2004. The president and the public: Inaugural addresses in American history. *Congress & the Presidency: A Journal of Capital Studies* 31. 21–52.
Kövecses, Zoltán. 2015. *Where metaphors come from: Reconsidering context in metaphor.* New York, NY: Oxford University Press.
Kövecses, Zoltán. 2020. *Extended conceptual metaphor theory.* Cambridge, England: Cambridge University Press.
Kubát, Miroslav & Radek Cech. 2016. Quantitative analysis of US presidential inaugural addresses. *Glottometrics* 34. 14–27.
Lapaire, Jean-Rémi. 2017. Grammaire cognitive des prépositions : Epistémologie et applications. *Corela* HS-(22). 1–25.
Lim, Elvin T. 2002. Five trends in presidential rhetoric: An analysis of rhetoric from George Washington to Bill Clinton. *Presidential Studies Quarterly.* Wiley Online Library 32(2). 328–348.
Lincoln, Abraham. 1861. First Inaugural Address. *The American Presidency Project.* https://www.presidency.ucsb.edu/documents/inaugural-address-34 (24 January, 2017).
Meyer, Michel. 2010. The Brussels School of rhetoric: From the new rhetoric to problematology. *Philosophy & Rhetoric.* JSTOR 43(4). 403–429.
Mieder, Wolfgang. 2001. "There is always a better tomorrow": Proverbial rhetoric in inaugural addresses by American presidents during the second half of the twentieth century. *Narodna Umjetnost* 38(1). 153–172.
Monroe, James. 1817. First Inaugural Address. *The American Presidency Project.* https://www.presidency.ucsb.edu/documents/inaugural-address-23 (24 January, 2017).
Monroe, James. 1821. Second Inaugural Address. *The American Presidency Project.* https://www.presidency.ucsb.edu/documents/inaugural-address-24 (24 January, 2017).
Nixon, Richard. 1969. First Inaugural Address. *The American Presidency Project.* https://www.presidency.ucsb.edu/documents/inaugural-address-1 (24 January, 2022).
Nixon, Richard. 1973. Second Inaugural Address. *The American Presidency Project.* https://www.presidency.ucsb.edu/documents/oath-office-and-second-inaugural-address (24 January, 2017).
Obama, Barack. 2009. First Inaugural Address. *The American Presidency Project.* https://www.presidency.ucsb.edu/documents/inaugural-address-5 (24 January, 2022).
Obama, Barack. 2013. Second Inaugural Address. *The American Presidency Project.* https://www.presidency.ucsb.edu/documents/inaugural-address-15 (24 January, 2017).
Pierce, Franklin. 1853. First Inaugural Address. *The American Presidency Project.* https://www.presidency.ucsb.edu/documents/inaugural-address-32 (24 January, 2017).

Polk, James K. 1845. First Inaugural Address. *The American Presidency Project.* https://www.presidency.ucsb.edu/documents/inaugural-address-30 (24 January, 2017).
Reagan, Ronald. 1981. First Inaugural Address. *The American Presidency Project.* https://www.presidency.ucsb.edu/documents/inaugural-address-11 (24 January, 2017).
Reagan, Ronald. 1985. Second Inaugural Address. *The American Presidency Project.* https://www.presidency.ucsb.edu/documents/inaugural-address-10 (24 January, 2017).
Roosevelt, Franklin D. 1933. First Inaugural Address. *The American Presidency Project.* https://www.presidency.ucsb.edu/documents/inaugural-address-8 (24 January, 2017).
Roosevelt, Franklin D. 1937. Second Inaugural Address. *The American Presidency Project.* https://www.presidency.ucsb.edu/documents/inaugural-address-7 (24 January, 2022).
Roosevelt, Franklin D. 1941. Third Inaugural Address. *The American Presidency Project.* https://www.presidency.ucsb.edu/documents/third-inaugural-address (24 January, 2017).
Roosevelt, Franklin D. 1945. Fourth Inaugural Address. *The American Presidency Project.* https://www.presidency.ucsb.edu/documents/inaugural-address-6 (24 January, 2017).
Schaffner, Christina. 1997. *Analysing political speeches.* Clevedon, England: Multilingual Matters.
Taft, William Howard. 1909. First Inaugural Address. *The American Presidency Project.* https://www.presidency.ucsb.edu/documents/inaugural-address-46 (24 January, 2017).
Taylor, Zachary. 1849. First Inaugural Address. *The American Presidency Project.* https://www.presidency.ucsb.edu/documents/inaugural-address-31 (24 January, 2017).
Trim, Richard. 2011. *Metaphor and the historical evolution of conceptual mapping.* Basingstoke, England: Palgrave Macmillan.
Truman, Harry S. 1949. First Inaugural Address. *The American Presidency Project.* https://www.presidency.ucsb.edu/documents/inaugural-address-4 (24 January, 2017).
van Buren, Martin. 1837. First Inaugural Address. *The American Presidency Project.* https://www.presidency.ucsb.edu/documents/inaugural-address-16 (24 January, 2017).
Washington, George. 1789. First Inaugural Address. *The American Presidency Project.* https://www.presidency.ucsb.edu/documents/inaugural-address-16 (24 January, 2017).
Washington, George. 1793. Second Inaugural Address. *The American Presidency Project.* https://www.presidency.ucsb.edu/documents/inaugural-address-17 (24 January, 2017).
Wilson, Woodrow. 1913. First Inaugural Address. *The American Presidency Project.* https://www.presidency.ucsb.edu/documents/inaugural-address-47 (24 January, 2022).
Wilson, Woodrow. 1917. Second Inaugural Address. *The American Presidency Project.* https://www.presidency.ucsb.edu/documents/inaugural-address-48 (24 January, 2017).
Zhang, Weiwei, Dirk Geeraerts & Dirk Speelman. 2015. Visualizing onomasiological change: Diachronic variation in metonymic patterns for WOMAN in Chinese. *Cognitive Linguistics.* De Gruyter 26(2). 289–330.

9 Concluding remarks

The present study is an attempt to examine the usages of metaphor-related prepositions in the American presidential inaugural addresses and explore their potential conceptual patterns, pragmatic functions, and diachronic variations. The forthcoming sections will address these dimensions by answering five specific questions.

9.1 How are prepositions distributed in the Inaugural Corpus?

Textbooks and even some scientific research treat prepositions as a homogenous group without specifying their frequencies in corpora. However, the findings of this corpus-based study paint a different picture. Interestingly, prepositions show sharp inequality in the three types of distributional frequency: frequency lists, co-occurrences, and dispersions. First, prepositions are unevenly distributed, with 11 prepositions accounting for 90.9% of all the occurrences of prepositions in the Inaugural Corpus. The high frequency of this specific set remains largely unaffected by any diachronic and idiosyncratic factors. Second, the preposition OF stands out, thanks to its exceptionally high frequency, warranting its own distinct category. In contrast, other categories encompass a considerably larger number of prepositions with relatively low frequencies. Some prepositions could be considered marginal, while some others are totally absent from the Inaugural Corpus. Finally, it has been observed that the frequency of prepositions has gradually declined over time. In the 18th and 19th centuries, the ratio was one preposition for every 5 words, while, in the 21st century, it decreased to one preposition for every 8 words. This decline in preposition usage can be seen as a stylistic marker, signaling a shift from a high degree of formality to a less formal and even informal communication style. The trend suggests that modern presidents tend to adopt a more casual and conversational tone in their direct communication with the people. It may also reflect a departure from the rigid formalities of the past and a shift to a more accessible and approachable language style.

DOI: 10.4324/9781003369646-9

9.2 What is the conceptual basis of metaphor-related prepositions?

Metaphor-related prepositions generate an emergent blend made up of two conceptual domains and a preposition that structures the relationship between them. This blend may profit from resemblance and correlation between these domains, but it is primarily constrained by the preposition's image schema. When used metaphorically, prepositions accentuate the relationships *within* these conceptual domains and generate metaphors based on correspondences between these relationships. For instance, these metaphors are based on cross-system mappings in which the inherent relationships of a natural or mechanical system are mapped onto a political system. In both these concrete and abstract systems, prepositions are vital to highlight particular relationships and to generate their associated inferences. These relational profiles serve a least three functions: (1) to characterize abstract concepts in terms of their distinctive relationships; (2) to rationalize their arguments via the image-schematic logic of these prepositions; and (3) to pass axiological evaluations by using the norms of these relationships as "sources of normativity" (Fairclough & Fairclough 2018: 174).

When considering the interaction between metaphor and metonymy, metaphor-related prepositions are motivated by metonymies. For example, the preposition OF evokes the PART-WHOLE image schema, which is inherently metonymic. In preposition-based mapping, a source domain is used to structure a given target domain through the metonymic basis of a particular preposition. This blend between a conceptual domain and a prepositional image schematic meaning gives rise to "metaphorical and metonymic coherence" (Barcelona 2009: 1).

In terms of conceptual notation, the standard formula typically includes two conceptual domains represented as A is B. For example, "the voice of the nation" is represented by THE NATION IS A PERSON. This formula takes nouns as the default part of speech in conceptual notations and, therefore, fails to incorporate the preposition OF. As the standard formula does not highlight the role of prepositions, it requires a revision of its notation system. A proper formula should focus on the preposition in order to reflect the correspondence between the concrete voice, as an intrinsic part of humans, and the nation's imaginary voice. In the revised notation system, this metaphor can be represented by the A OF B formula.

9.3 How do metaphor-related prepositions mix?

Most metaphor-related prepositions tend to appear in a coherent cluster of metaphors. These clusters are of two types. The first type includes multiple prepositions, such as the FROM-TO construction, while the second type includes a metaphor-related preposition with another metaphor expressed by another part of speech. In both types, the tendency is toward coherence more than clash. As the inaugurals are well-drafted texts, it seems that their writers are aware that "mixed metaphors are cognitively successful" (Kimmel 2010: 110), and they, therefore, invest considerable time and effort in carefully blending metaphors and ensuring their coherence. This coherence is achieved through the integration of underlying image schemas, as explained by Mandler and Cánovas (2014: 528), which allows language users to process adjacent metaphors.

9.4 Do metaphor-related prepositions reflect any systematic conceptualizations?

This study's findings suggest that the seemingly unrelated metaphorical senses of the prepositions can result in a coherent cognitive model. Within this model, metaphor-related prepositions are purposefully employed to create a unified conceptualization of political concepts and actions in two major processes: conceptual identity and conceptual space. In the first process, political concepts and actions are defined by their salient features via the intrinsic relationships of some prepositions, such as OF and WITH. In the second process, political concepts and actions are characterized via the prepositions' schematic relationships by locating them in a conceptual space within three different frames of reference: location, direction, and extent.

These two processes reflect particular representations of reality extracted from "certain features and relations from whatever it's representing" (Tversky 2018: 59). As the metaphor-related prepositions are (part of) the presidents' construal of reality, this cognitive model shapes and is shaped by "cognitive associations in the minds of language users" (Schmid & Küchenhoff 2013: 532).

9.5 How do metaphor-related prepositions vary across history?

As far as the diachronic dimension is concerned, the findings reveal that both stability and change factors have an impact on metaphor variations. As American presidents are expected to evoke "continuity with provocation, endorsing established ideas while simultaneously advancing new ones" (Martin 2015: 28), their use of metaphor-related prepositions reflects this oscillation between stable conceptualizations and novel ones.

Factors of stability include the following: (1) prepositions form a closed group with stable membership; (2) the meanings of the prepositions are constant because of their image schema; (3) cross-system mappings create inertia by which stable mappings persist; (4) American presidents are expected to rehearse a specific set of timeless principles, and (5) inaugurals have developed stable generic properties. Combined, these factors generate

Concluding remarks 103

entrenched metaphors, eventually resulting in "stable mapping templates" (Canovas 2014: 296). Replicating these templates is likely to establish consistent patterns and enhance the "cumulative effect" of these constant and recurring conceptual mappings (Bybee 2007). Due to their prolonged entrenchment, metaphors become more prone to disseminate "a rhetoric of obviousness" (Meyer 2010: 414). However, significant events, influential innovations, emerging needs, and novel ways of thinking, among other factors, pose challenges to replicating identical templates.

Incentives of change are created by the following factors: (1) the changing relationship between American presidents and their people, (2) paradigmatic shifts, (3) the potential of the prepositions to create new parameters, (4) the idiosyncratic style and character of each president and their passion for distinction, and (5) the impact of cultural and historical circumstances.

Metaphor-related prepositions used throughout the Inaugural Corpus are caught between these stabilizing factors and the provocative change factors. In one way, an inaugural address can be considered the speech of the victorious who writes history, but at the same, this address is expected to disseminate the same old concepts. Each president has to tell their unique version of the new history, but they also have to reiterate older versions of timeless history. In both cases, it is the history of the nation, the state, the political system, the people, and the character of the victorious presidents who "invite us to see them, the presidency, and the country's role in specific ways", as Campbell and Jamieson (1985) put it.

9.6   Final words

Taken together, my findings suggest that prepositions are much more than space indicators, and they "cannot be characterized solely in terms of spatial configuration" (Langacker 2010: 1). Instead, metaphor-related prepositions can incorporate various nonspatial elements coherently, thanks to their intrinsic and schematic relationships. As relators, these prepositions serve to dissolve the semantic tension caused by the seemingly incompatible entities in metaphorical relationships. The outcome is a "new congruence", or "new semantic pertinence", to borrow Ricœur's words, which may reflect the vividness of imagery. The new relationships created by the preposition-based metaphors reveal our capacity for conceptual integration. The emergent blends are coherently structured by a conceptual model that incorporates culture and cognition and situates metaphors and metonymies in their sociocultural contexts.

In addition, recurring preposition-based metaphors and metonymies demonstrate, at least partially, that political language is an integral part of political reality. By replicating metaphors of the political system, politicians craft reassuring messages to the public concerning their shared interests, expectations, and future. In these messages, judgments are passed through "ideologically attitudinal" prepositions (Goatly 2006: 16), empowered by the modern state's coercive authority via the coercive voice of its president or the modern Peitho, the goddess of persuasion according to Greek mythology. The overall outcome is a prescriptive discourse that promotes the state's supremacy and presupposes the people's obedience. The tools of this coercive power are naturalizing arguments and fatalist realism hammered by preposition-based metaphors and metonymies. Their conceptual mappings emphasize normalization and naturalization and give the impression that the state is organic and, therefore, part of the prevailing doxa. For example, the metaphorical OF tends to associate with source domains that propagate "a supposed naturalness" (Chilton & Schaffner 2011: 321) whenever political concepts are either defined or described.

These findings contribute to the body of research on metaphorical patterns in presidential rhetoric. Current research on political thoughts can benefit from studying how metaphor-related prepositions evoke the underlying structure of political concepts and improve the "efficacy of presidential communication" (Scacco & Coe 2016: 2017). These metaphors gain extra rhetorical weight because they are delivered by the nation's leaders whose inaugurals are chapters within the narratives of the victorious presidents, seamlessly merging into the timeless annals of history.

Further research is needed to characterize the metaphorical usages of prepositions in other discourses and genres. Gamson et al. (1992: 381) argue that "a whole set of texts may have an even more invisible metamessage". Specific corpora are more likely to reveal only a part of the usages of metaphor-related prepositions, especially with the increasing fragmentation of reality.

In addition, corpora in languages other than English offer valuable areas of exploration where prepositions of different languages can be compared and contrasted to explore the lines that separate universal principles from cultural variations. As new meanings continue to emerge out of the "recurring patterns of engagement between organism and environment" (Johnson & Lakoff 2002: 248), new studies are still required to explore "the culturally-defined metaphoric language in contrast to the kinds of universal trends" (Trim 2007: 49).

American presidents have not only delivered addresses full of metaphors, but they themselves have become metaphors for their nations. Their power has been forged through the weight of their words, including the prepositions they have carefully selected. Further work needs to be conducted to explore the various aspects of meaning-making, considering that "meaning is never universal, total, neutral, or permanent" (Taylor 2005: 131) and to support the ongoing investigation of "meaning, conceptualization, reason, knowledge, truth, and language" (Johnson & Lakoff 2002: 245).

With advances in digital texts, public political discourse may undergo more transformations in its content and format by the ever-growing information technologies. Classical concepts such as author, authoring, reader, reading, and space are about to be redefined, and "a global or delocalized circulation of discourse" has become commonplace (Kirby 2015: 76). How will future American presidents respond to the delocalization of discourse and the placelessness of cyberspace, while also addressing the constraints of the nation-state-geography localism? These endeavors will undoubtedly demand rigorous exploration and analysis. Within the same futurist line of thought, we may wonder whether political discourse will exist without vivid metaphors. This futurist remark is not a new hypothesis. It is built on a warning drawn from the "fallacy of misplaced concreteness", posited by Alfred North Whitehead. Instead of deciphering political metaphors and making sense of their meanings and inferences, figurative language may obscure the complexities of political realities through excessive or shallow concreteness. Post-postmodernist patterns will likely generate new inertia "suited to producing safe speeches than great speeches" (Collier 2014: 23).

References

Barcelona, Antonio. 2009. The metaphorical and metonymic understanding of the Trinitarian dogma. *International Journal of English Studies* 3(1). 1–28.

Bybee, Joan L. 2007. Diachronic linguistics. In Geeraerts, Dirk & Cuyckens, Hubert (ed.), *The Oxford handbook of cognitive linguistics*, 945–987. New York, NY: Oxford University Press.

Campbell, Karlyn Kohrs & Kathleen Hall Jamieson. 1985. Inaugurating the presidency. *Presidential Studies Quarterly* 15(2). 394–411.

Canovas, Cristobal Pagan. 2014. Cognitive patterns in Greek poetic metaphors of emotion: A diachronic approach. In Vera, Javier E. Diaz (ed.), *Metaphor and metonymy across time and cultures: Perspectives on the sociohistorical linguistics of figurative language*, 295–318. Berlin, Germany: De Gruyter.

Chilton, Paul & Christina Schaffner. 2011. Discourse and politics. In Van Dijk, Teun A. (ed.), *Discourse studies: A multidisciplinary introduction*, 303–330. London, England: Sage.

Collier, Ken. 2014. Rhetoric and representation: Exploring the institutionalization of presidential speechwriting. In *Southern Political Science Association Meeting*, 1–32. New Orleans, LA: Southern Political Science Association.

Fairclough, Norman & Isabela Fairclough. 2018. A procedural approach to ethical critique in CDA. *Critical Discourse Studies*. Taylor & Francis 15(2). 169–185.

Gamson, William A., David Croteau, William Hoynes & Theodore Sasson. 1992. Media images and the social construction of reality. *Annual Review of Sociology* 18. 373–393.

Goatly, Andrew. 2006. Humans, animals, and metaphors. *Society \& Animals*. Brill 14(1). 15–37.

Johnson, Mark & George Lakoff. 2002. Why cognitive linguistics requires embodied realism. *Cognitive Linguistics* 13(3). 245–264.

Kimmel, Michael. 2010. Why we mix metaphors (and mix them well): Discourse coherence, conceptual metaphor, and beyond. *Journal of Pragmatics*. Elsevier 42(1). 97–115.

Kirby, Alan. 2015. The possibility of cyber-placelessness digimodernism on a planetary platform. In Elias, Amy J. & Moraru, Christian (ed.), *The planetary turn:*

Relationality and geoaesthetics in the twenty-first century, 71–88. Evanston, IS: Northwestern University Press.
Langacker, Ronald W. 2010. Reflections on the functional characterization of spatial prepositions. *Corela* HS-(7). 1–20.
Mandler, Jean M. & Cristóbal Pagán Cánovas. 2014. On defining image schemas. *Language and Cognition* 6(4). 510–532.
Martin, James. 2015. Situating speech: A rhetorical approach to political strategy. *Political Studies* 63(1). 25–42.
Meyer, Michel. 2010. The Brussels School of rhetoric: From the new rhetoric to problematology. *Philosophy & Rhetoric*. JSTOR 43(4). 403–429.
Scacco, Joshua M. & Kevin Coe. 2016. The ubiquitous presidency: Toward a new paradigm for studying presidential communication. *International Journal of Communication* 10. 2014–2037.
Schmid, Hans-Jörg & Helmut Küchenhoff. 2013. Collostructional analysis and other ways of measuring lexicogrammatical attraction: Theoretical premises, practical problems and cognitive underpinnings. *Cognitive Linguistics* 24(3). 531–577.
Taylor, Bryan C. 2005. Postmodern theory. In *Engaging organizational communication theory and research: Multiple perspectives*, 113–140. Thousand Oaks, CA: Sage.
Trim, Richard. 2007. Culture-specific conceptualisation. In *Metaphor networks: The comparative evolution of figurative language*, 49–62. Basingstoke, England: Palgrave Macmillan.
Tversky, Barbara. 2018. Multiple models. In the mind and in the world. *Historical Social Research Supplement* 31. 59–65.

Index

analog: analogical 15, 16, 28; analogies 15; analogy 16, 21, 22, 32, 33, 71, 84, 97
Aristotle 21, 32, 37, 48, 96
axiological 17, 19, 78, 101

Cicero 22, 37
Civil Rights 63, 91, 93, 96
civil war 62, 77, 88
civilization 89, 93
cognitive grammar 5, 7, 13, 19, 71
cognitive model 30, 73, 83, 96, 102
Cold War 38, 90, 96
commercial transactions 61, 62
community 2, 16, 35, 59, 61, 75, 94
conflict 37, 42, 43, 65
Congress 39, 43, 98
Constitution 41, 43, 64, 75, 87
container 14, 15, 31, 41, 42, 60, 77
contextualization: context 2, 4, 15, 16, 17, 18, 19, 23, 26, 29, 30, 33, 36, 40, 45, 46, 52, 70, 92, 94, 96, 98; contexts 15, 17, 25, 30, 35, 91, 103; contextual 4, 5, 16, 17, 30, 31
conversational 34, 39, 43, 44, 56, 100
corpus-based 1, 5, 18, 50, 100
correlation 11, 56, 101
cross-system mapping 61, 62, 63

darkness 42, 59, 61, 65, 69, 74, 75, 78, 82, 90
deity: God 23, 41, 78; goddess 36, 104
deliberation 35, 36
democrat: democracy 42, 65, 80, 91, 92; democratic 35, 43, 44, 75, 78; undemocratic 36, 75, 79, 92
diachronic variations 6, 73, 87, 93, 100
diseases 61, 89, 90, 91

distribution 5, 6, 35, 51, 52, 53, 54
dynamism: dynamic 7, 10, 14, 17, 29, 31, 51, 77, 80; dynamics 11, 16, 29, 34, 63

eloquence 7, 23, 24, 37
embody: embodied 20, 23, 30, 33; embodiment 30, 34, 45, 46
emotionality: emotion 36, 37, 42, 75, 80, 84, 105; emotional 2, 11, 12, 37, 38, 87, 91; emotions 11, 14, 35, 36, 37, 40, 74, 78, 79, 87
Enlightenment 23
entrenched 11, 28, 39, 103
environment 30, 42, 65, 104
Era of Good Feelings 87, 93
evolutionary 45

family 42, 59, 61, 68, 74, 75, 88, 93, 94
father 68, 75, 88
Federalist Era 87, 93
figurative 1, 2, 3, 4, 17, 18, 21, 68, 71, 78, 81, 105
force 11, 13, 14, 25, 63, 74
formality 56, 100
formula 70, 101
freedom 4, 19, 61, 63, 64, 80, 82, 90, 93
front-back 41, 66

generic properties 39, 40, 46, 56, 94, 102
Gilded Age 89, 93
Great Depression 90, 93, 96

happiness 76, 80, 81, 87, 93
health 42, 74
hierarchies: hierarchical 4, 12; hierarchy 29, 31, 41, 66
Hobbes, T. 24
human body 30, 42, 59, 61, 67

Index

image schemata: schema 14, 15, 24, 25, 31, 41, 42, 67, 74, 79, 81, 87, 92, 101, 102; schemas 5, 7, 14, 19, 20, 30, 31, 32, 34, 42, 66, 72, 87, 94, 102, 106; schematic 13, 14, 15, 18, 20, 28, 31, 45, 60, 66, 69, 70, 77, 94, 101, 102, 103; schematicity 29
inertia 63, 94, 102, 105
inferences 5, 16, 47, 75, 77, 78, 101, 105

Jacksonian Era 88, 93
Jeffersonian Era 88, 93
journeys 42, 59, 61, 65
justice 50, 61, 87, 89, 91, 92, 93

Kant 24, 33, 81

liberty 4, 43, 61, 75, 76, 80, 87, 93

media 35, 39, 44, 48, 56, 57
metonym: metonymic 6, 14, 15, 18, 29, 32, 49, 58, 66, 68, 69, 71, 74, 99, 101, 105; metonymies 5, 15, 30, 42, 57, 66, 69, 73, 101, 103, 104; metonymy 17, 18, 29, 30, 32, 67, 69, 71, 77, 101
mixed metaphors 63, 64, 102
modernist 79, 80, 96
morals: moral 16, 18, 36, 42, 76, 78, 79, 80, 90; morality 17, 38
motion 41, 59, 77, 79, 80, 82, 85, 90
music 61, 75, 94

narration: narrative 31; narratives 38, 73, 104
natural phenomena 42, 69, 76, 94
naturalness 62, 89, 104
Nietzsche, F. 25
norms 17, 62, 95, 101
notation 6, 69, 101

orators 22, 37
orientational 4, 17

Part-whole 31
peace 42, 63, 76, 80, 87
Peitho 36, 104
persuasiveness: persuade 2, 36, 44, 62, 89; persuasion 33, 36, 37, 44, 48, 104; persuasive 1, 7, 36, 39

Plato 21, 33, 36
poetry 21
political communication 35, 37, 38, 47, 49
political culture 43, 61, 94, 95
political language 35, 36, 103
political metaphors 6, 41, 61, 62, 63, 94, 105
polyseme: polysemous 11; polysemy 10, 11, 16, 19
postmodernist 71, 84, 96, 97, 105
Pragglejaz Group 3, 59
prepositional 1, 2, 3, 10, 14, 50, 101
preposition-based metaphors 15, 64, 70, 103
presidential communication 6, 43, 104, 106
Progressive Era 89, 93
propaganda 36, 49
proportional reasoning 15, 16
prosperity 65, 80, 81, 90, 93
public opinion 6, 36, 38, 39, 44

ratio 24, 55, 100
Reconstruction Era 88, 93
reference point 4, 13
relators 4, 5, 103
republic 60, 65
Roaring Twenties 89, 93

Scriptures 23, 75
semantic fields 5, 45, 59, 60, 94
semantics 15, 17, 20, 26, 32, 48, 94
sociocultural 5, 103
socioeconomic 16, 70, 79, 89
spirit 69, 75, 82, 91, 93
stability 6, 35, 40, 68, 71, 84, 93, 94, 95, 97, 102
substitution 21, 22, 25, 26

transference 21, 22, 24

unity 40, 75, 88
universal 30, 45, 104
up-down 41, 66

verticality 14, 60, 66, 79, 90

water 60, 62, 68, 76, 87, 92
weather 42, 68, 76
World War 89, 93

For Product Safety Concerns and Information please contact our EU representative GPSR@taylorandfrancis.com
Taylor & Francis Verlag GmbH, Kaufingerstraße 24, 80331 München, Germany

www.ingramcontent.com/pod-product-compliance
Lightning Source LLC
Chambersburg PA
CBHW051756230426
43670CB00012B/2311